the last american icon
emael

a daily meditation guide

Portions of this book appeared in The Drama Review published by
MIT Press Journals.

published by·
the house of emael
www.loveemael.com

images, cover photographs & book design by:
diego pacheco
postminimalwork
www.postminimal.com

ISBN 978-0-9797252-0-3

To María for introducing me to the work of Ralph Ellison;
and to invisible [people] everywhere.

preface

A great deal has happened at every imaginable level of human existence since the conception of this book in the year 2000. Initially, the idea was simply to chronicle/document my life as a performance artist for the complete year of 2001 by writing a haiku a day as a formal exercise/experiment; not only did I believe that such an endeavor would better discipline me in ways that would carry over into other areas of my life, but more importantly I wanted to offer people a strategy for reflecting on one's life on a daily basis. This seems even more necessary today than it did only seven years ago.

It is hard to talk about this book without addressing the great deal of pain and heartache surrounding the destruction of the World Trade Center on September 11, 2001. No matter how one attempts to explain this tragedy or the brutality that continues in its aftermath, the amount of suffering has been staggering and it would be to our credit as human beings if we could begin to envision a world together free of such atrocities.

A year and a half after 9-11, in the Summer of 2003, I was visiting with two important teachers who were working on a musical event together; family, friends and fellow artists were invited to *Pass the Peace*, where one could dance and celebrate being alive openly, conscious of the fact that part of the proceeds raised that evening would go "directly to various peace and community service agencies." While I sat in their living room that day as they worked through the details for the event in an impromptu meeting, I had the chance to pick up a particular copy of a Sylvia Browne book from the coffee table, called, The Otherside and Back; I had never read any of her work prior to that moment. Without much thought,

I opened the book to page 271 and read, "Separate governments will ultimately give way to a single global government." Given everything that had happened in recent years and that I was sitting in on a development meeting about *Peace* essentially, I tried to imagine from this perspective how a single global government might arise and what our world would look like after generations of such a movement. This is the inspiration for the title of the book.

This book is offered as a guide to help the reader meditate on living peacefully together on this planet and it is nothing else. If there is to be a global government, let it be: one based on harmony, love and peace. The invitation to imagine what The Last American Icon is or might look like under such considerations is ultimately one left to the reader's willingness and/or desire to live in such a world.

A small word of caution. As with all guide books, some of the information within these pages is either already (out)dated or quite possibly dangerous terrain for some people to explore. There is no way around this issue. Rather than edit the work to reflect contemporary global urban culture or my personal internal process, I have decided to leave the manuscript in its original form, allowing for critical discussion of the work in all its dimensions.

It is with great pleasure and gratitude that this book is released into the world. May it reach the hearts of courageous hands.

With love,
emael

December 2007

honeysuckle friends
sharing family stories,
our time is present

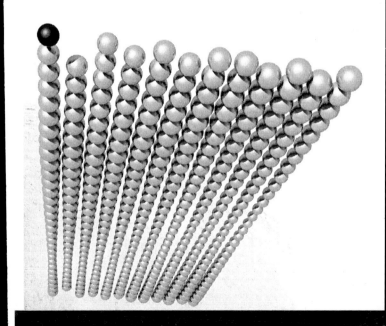

deep [home songs]* steady,
infused with each other's scent,
evening trains our goal
* house beats

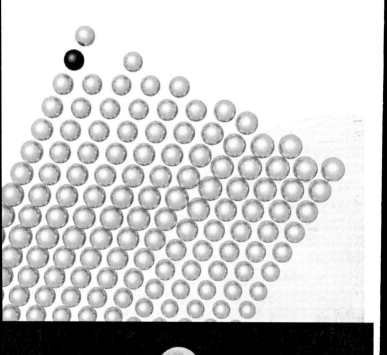

not only in dreams
hybridized butch-femme divines
coincidences

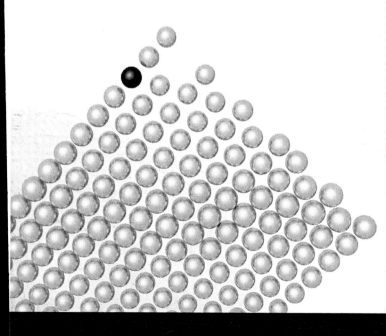

committing to self
connecting stars atop stairs
limbers stagnant thoughts

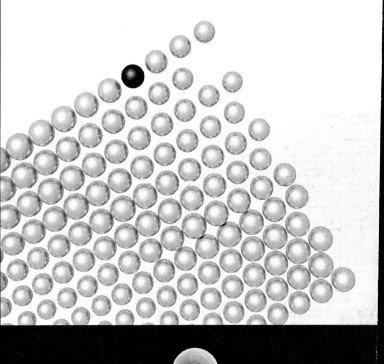

moon shines on shaved heads
hanging on red street corners,
fingers sorting sand

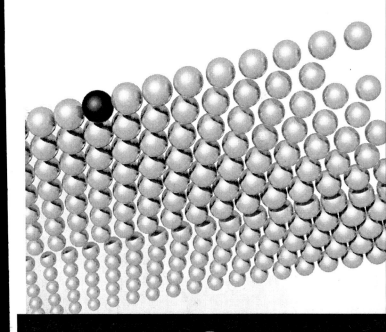

talk interests fade
before an act of nature
re-adjusts my eyes

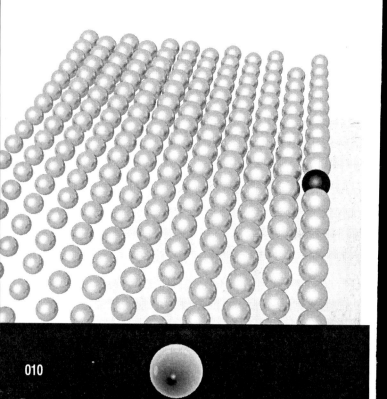

five friends feast fondly
atop audile attention
gathering ghettos

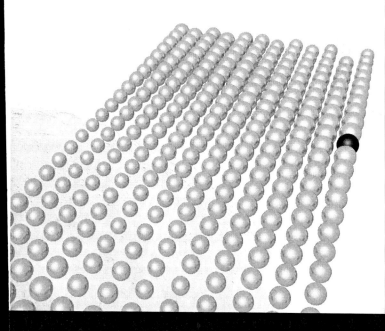

under the influx,
heteronormative films
pacify desire

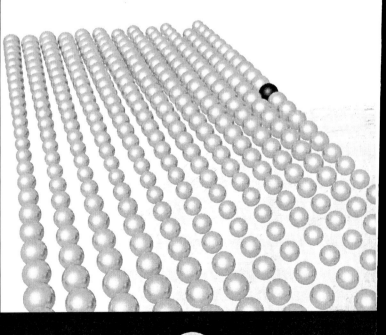

assimilation*
under late capitalism
makes the rich richer
* *or*, appropriation

i would like to think
about something other than
pain or oppression

the trouble with hair
so manageable, "white" folk
hate to accept it

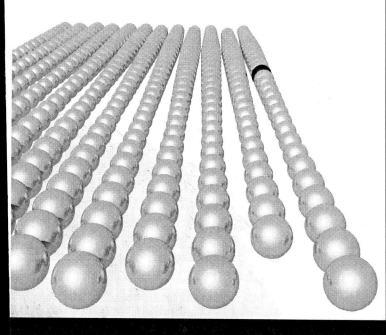

to avoid sadness,
best to not deter wind chime
from being itself

in moments of doubt:
everything i work towards
cannot be held back

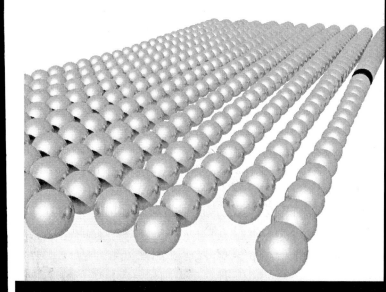

when asking an ant,
"can you teach me anything?"
it just kept scouting

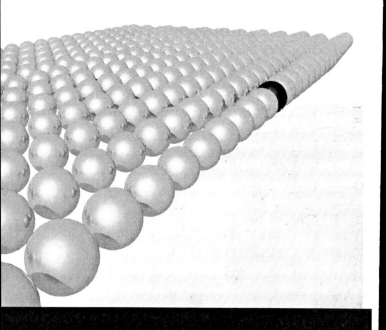

takes fifteen minutes
to begin to settle down
without any drugs

fuck conformity
and the lip service we pay
to equality*
* *or*, diversity

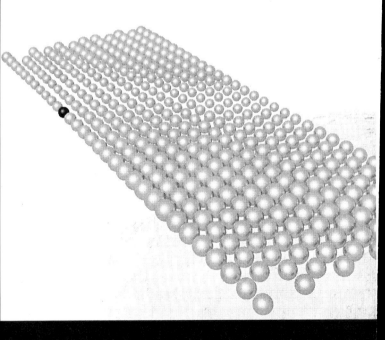

healing reactions
often deter radicals
who are unprepared

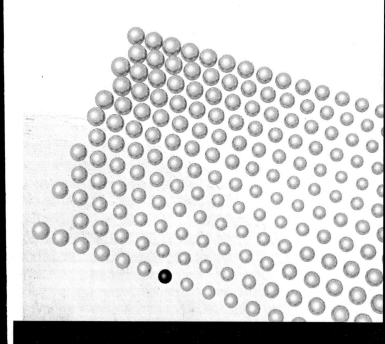

red feathers surround
a film reel while i ponder
public/private space

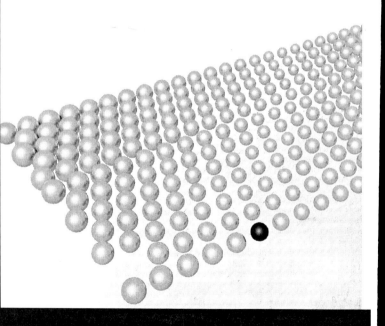

light traces appear
in a moment of darkness
and forge a new path

unhinging exp'tions
increases vitality
through urban body

concert human rights
conceptualism before
american me

sometimes an earthquake's
needed to get out of bed
and enjoy the day

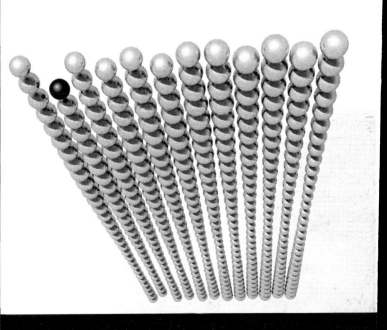

when violence strikes
a sister you love player,
who ain't a hater?

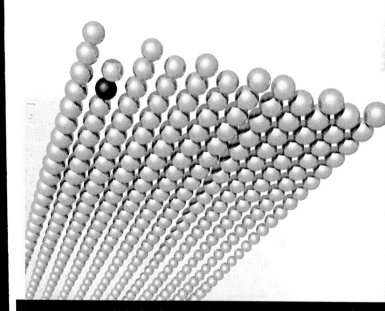

in isolation
i contemplate intentions
of art supporters

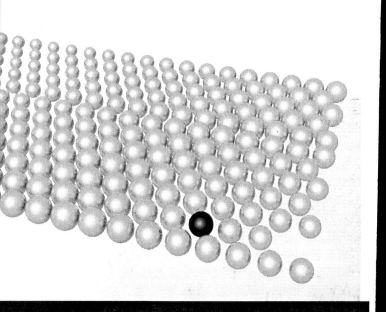

coalitions weave
patiently around warm food
and plenty of talk

by chance two friends sit
recovering memory
and defining roles

fifteen urinals
field vital politics in/
outside master's house

"new" trajectories
saturate culture squeezing
lemons from horses

transformers gather
tables around brown voices
ready for lift-off

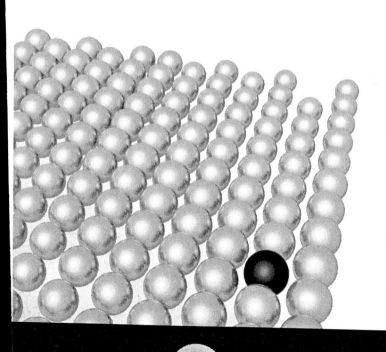

mestizos engage
apparitions of women
with fierce tostadas

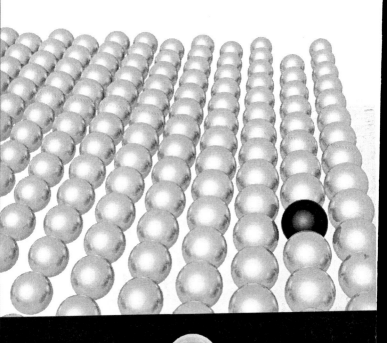

cross-over-dresser's
success begins with this tongue
licking frying pans

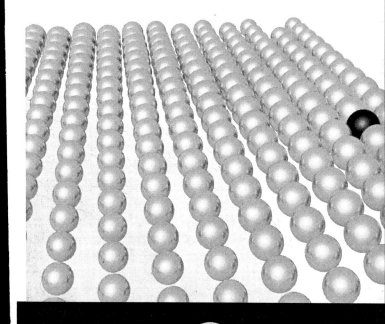

nuclear buttons
set off by self-indulgence
undermine women

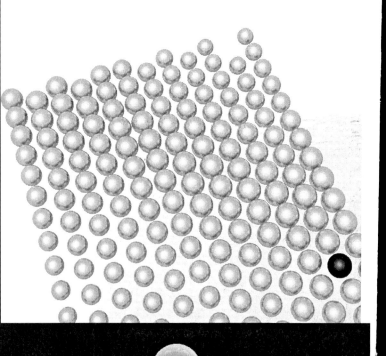

interstate terrain
swifts visions of whole rainbows
as friends theorize

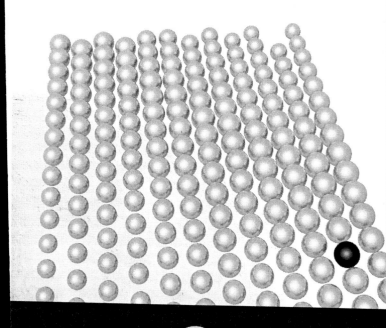

spacing traces near
centers and outskirts revolve
around affection

internal s(h)ifting
flowers vast capacities
charged with potential

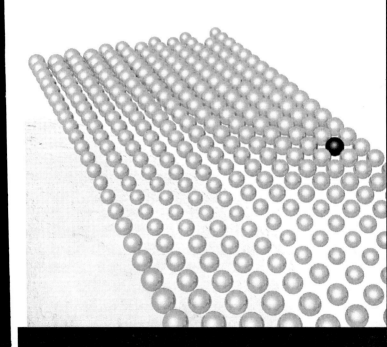

vague cosmic gestures
transport individuals
intending kinship

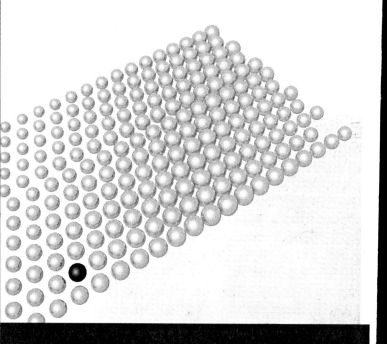

moments created
in fields of fragrant desire
appear above dawn

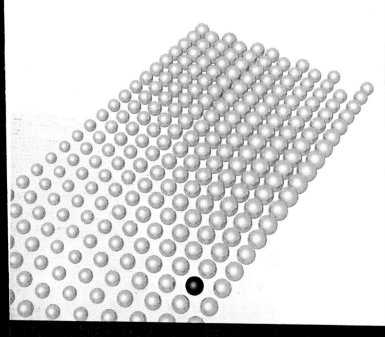

"normal" people watch
with or without friends present
until lights go out

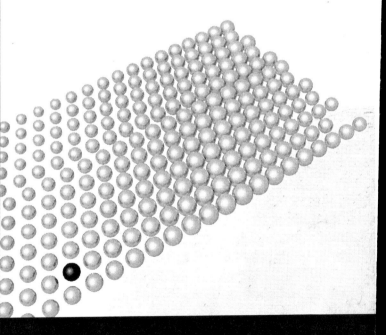

integrative texts
dissolve information files
organic-ally

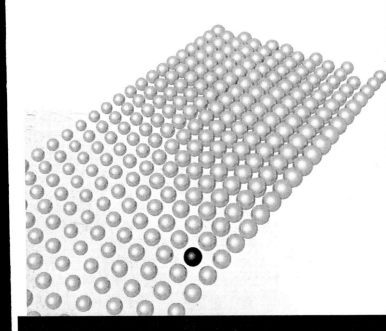

gentle thoughts open
andy's tomato soup can
finding another

blood works soft structures
subverting terminal blows
while sharing popcorn

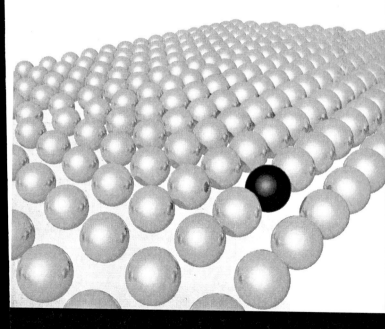

it's you but not you
intimating neon fears
of "gay's no future"

saged kitchen table
releases toxic thought streams
prepared "under god"

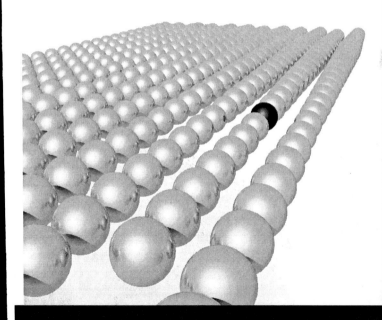

plastic dreams flashback
clay pot and jade mask remnants
collapsing time code

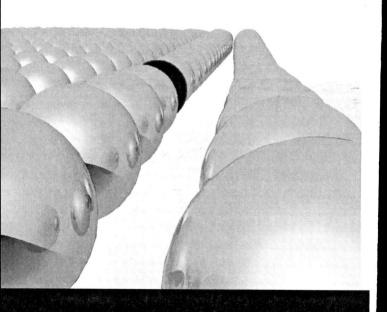

ceremony group
expels internalized pain
despite the police

raza blood thick eyes
eagerly scan brave world views
half naked but warm

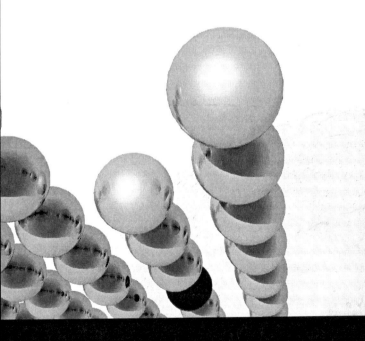

midnight breadths evoke
strong commitments to loved ones
in multi-verses

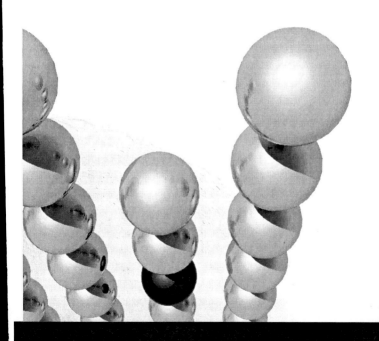

jails keep bars and walls
for colonizers "ready"
just in case we get...

corporate worldcon
assembles wireless racists
as lame as its parts

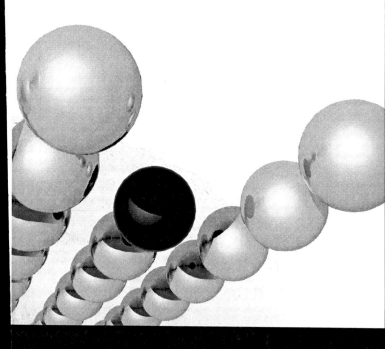

trans-lectual souls
knit while sharing history
the whole afternoon

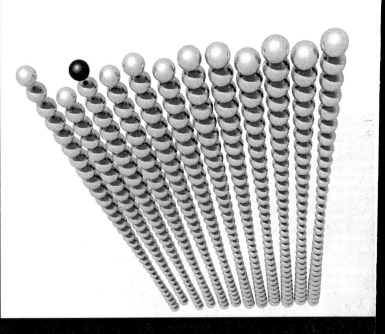

buddha baby brings
family spheres together
on long drives at dusk

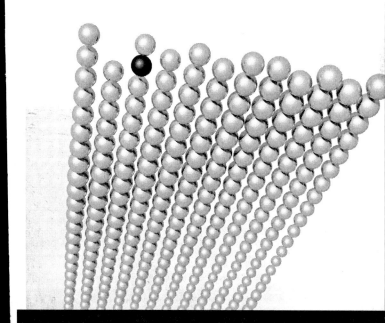

charged conversations
on unlearning violence
involve 'family'

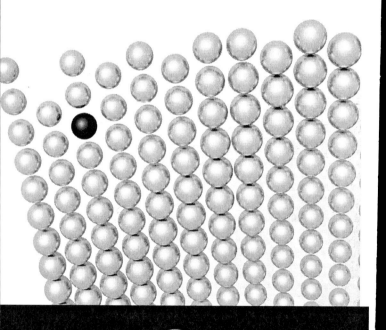

as post-enemies
we would require trust and faith
in non-violence

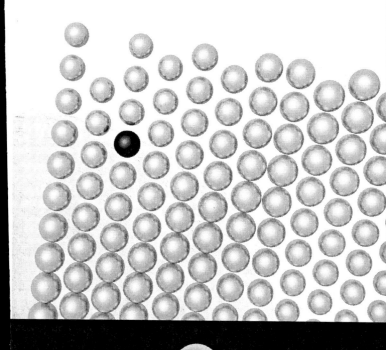

private surrender
on kitchen floor politics
calms me the way down

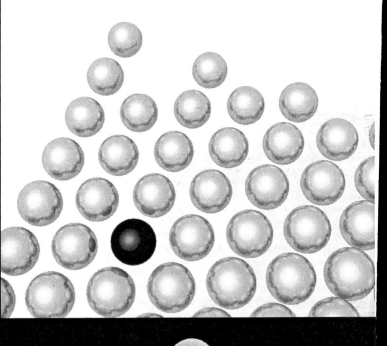

concrete plastic throws
chile fires out my rectum
lips fully exposed

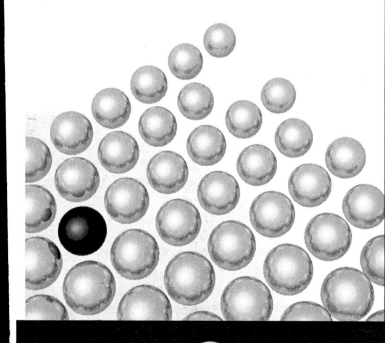

incredible sea
of men dance fashionably
over and over

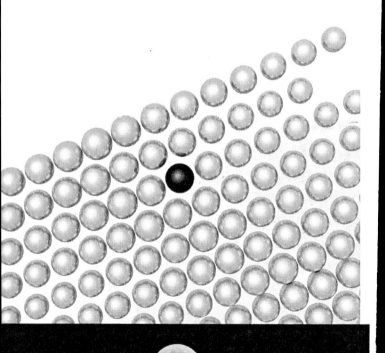

blissful "domestic"
severs ties with self-hatred
through performance rite

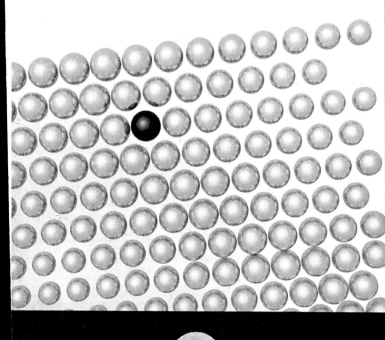

báe roots echo
octaves on resistant walls
affirming movement

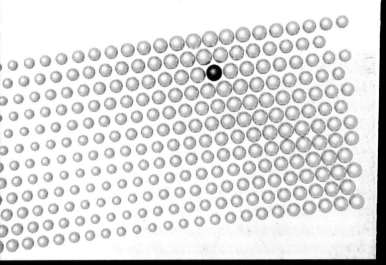

post-neo fashion
settings require quick escapes
from all that you know

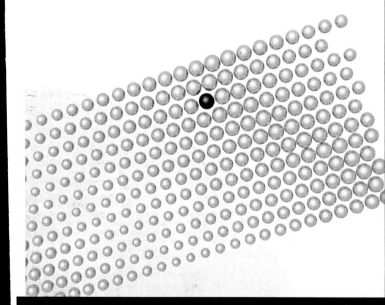

shifting perspectives
gather tele-space sound beats
transmitting wisdom

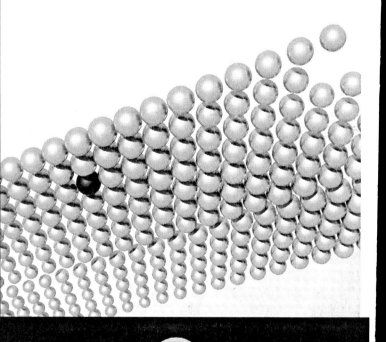

co(s)mic transcriptions
flutter loosely upon planes
awaiting request

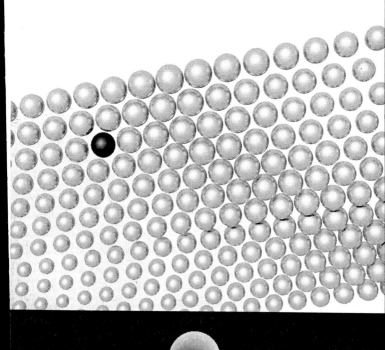

buscando letras
sobre mi escritorio
recién casadas

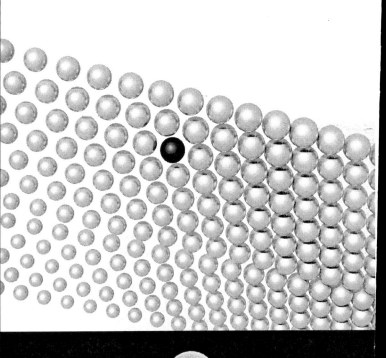

waves crash with shoes off
writing memories in sand
and making new friends

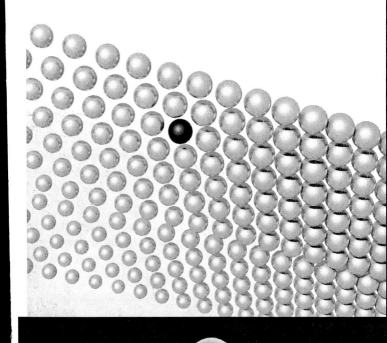

leaping hearts and smiles
full of love like no other
you fill me with song

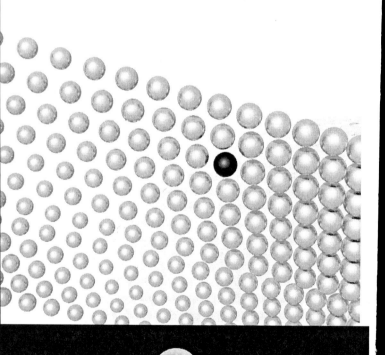

urban landscaping
conceptual beats and frames
i weave through downtown

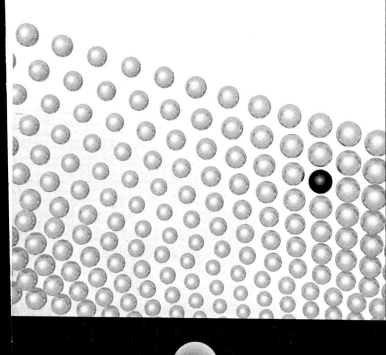

ultradown homegirl
hooks it up bigtime for real
along with a smile

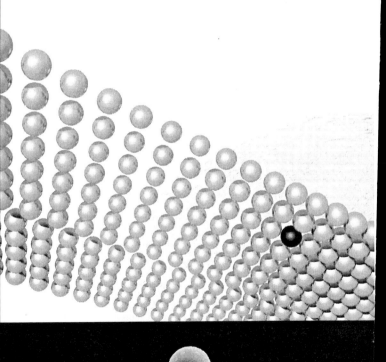

fog horns and sirens
sound while meditating on
being a good friend

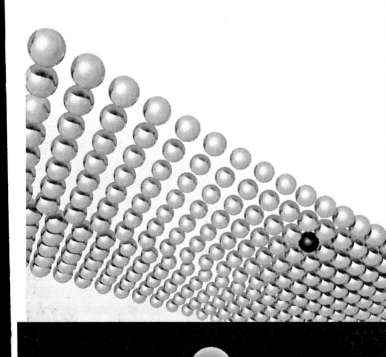

love supreme hits home
as la jotería swims
through my whole body

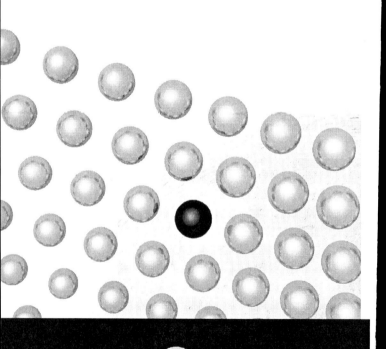

love significance
in mobile private spaces
straight up now tell me

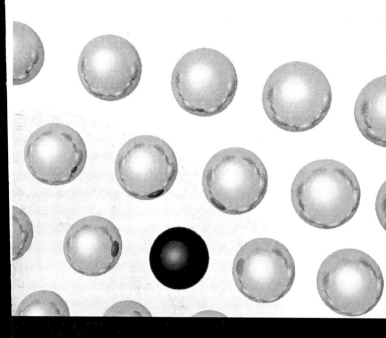

orange down that swirl
'round multiple deities
share knowledge of roots

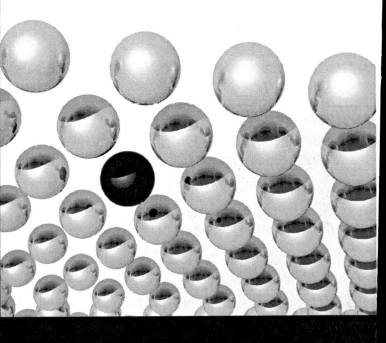

wind rattling dry leaves
brings images of loved ones
to mind before sleep

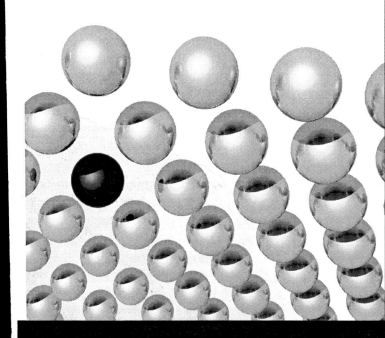

present moment breadth
expands my lungs completely
upon empty shelf

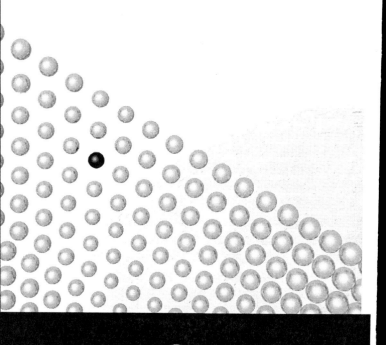

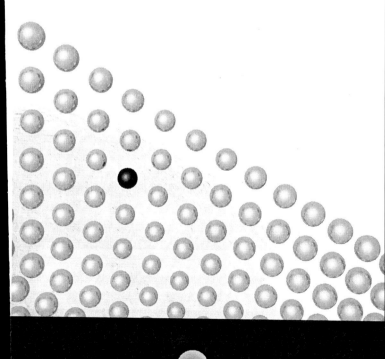

crow feather morning
sweeps clouds above blades of grass
conversing of love

bound to la vida
que me mantiene breathing,
i nourish me whole

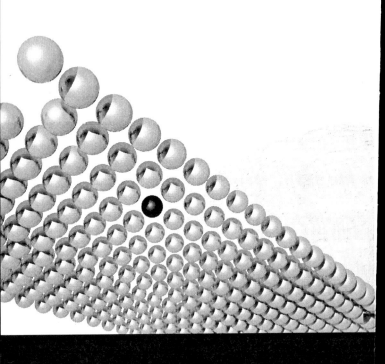

super hybridized
peeps the inner hood, we do
what we gotta do

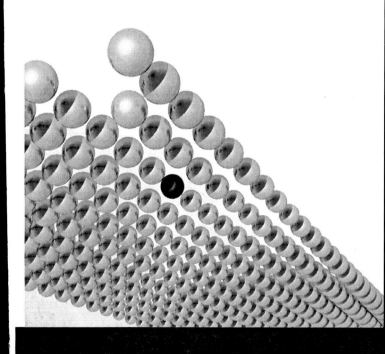

with our tongues untied,
"bent over in wet ditches"
cries from twisted lips

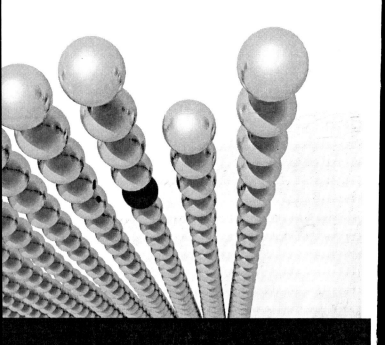

licking organic
mango from lips and fingers
peaks night with good friends

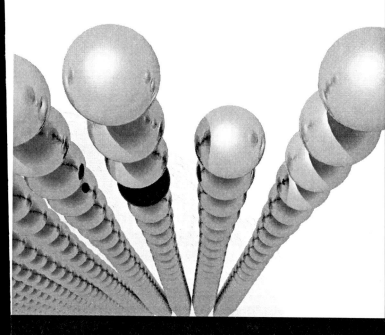

nothing floats over
head for a second and then
an airplane flies by

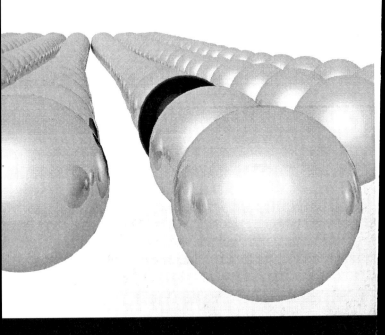

performance friendships
nourish one's entire being
from the beginning

intuition drives
this raza from hither to
exactly the place

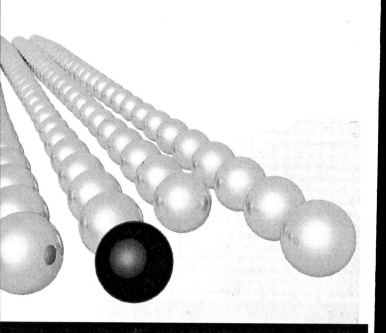

a friend with flowers
appears at my door first thing,
welcoming a smile

peaceful pen glides smooth
over paper as light bulb
shines atop my head

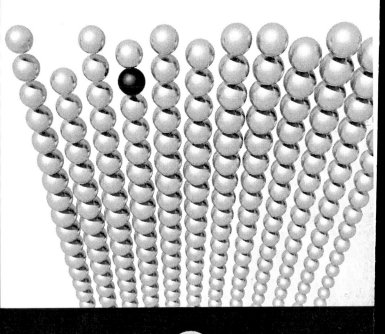

siempre con (c)alma
do i approach my writing,
otherwise it sucks

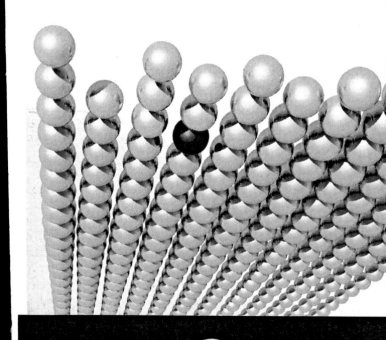

double sight flutters
on screen off-set by local
political scene

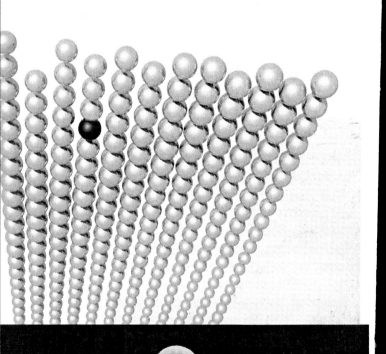

through medi(t)ation
resolutions are achieved
with understanding

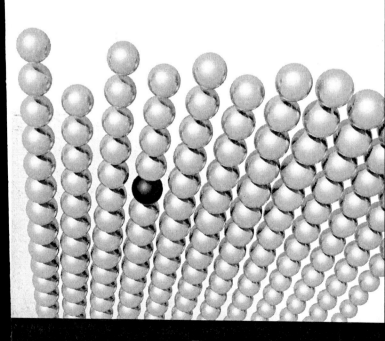

tenacious thought streams
subside during exertion
of earthly vessel

censoring people
rarely quiets anyone
who wants to be heard

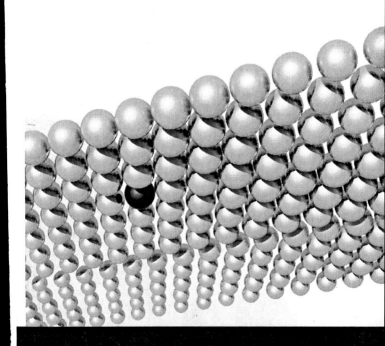

day was great until
two carloads of white young men
verbally attacked

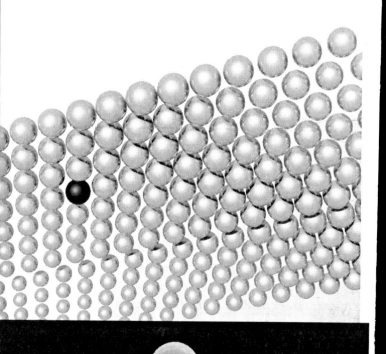

grounded flowers bloom
with a little bit of warmth
and mindful caring

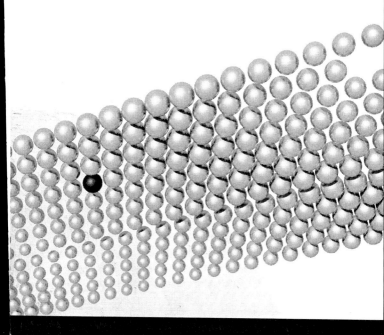

so post-colonial
relations depend vastly
on the personal

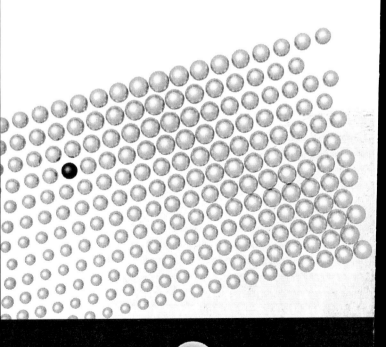

resignations cease
upon emptying notions
of limited gifts

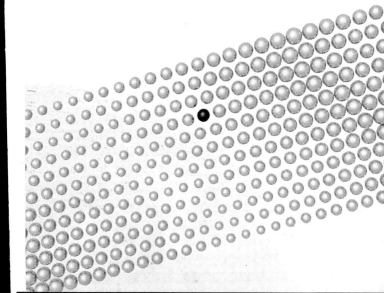

inviting love in
all forms into my writing
signals m'ew music

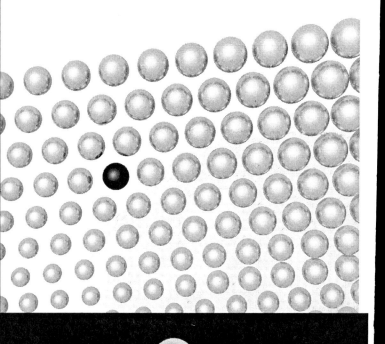

fame on my own terms
involves family and friends
working together

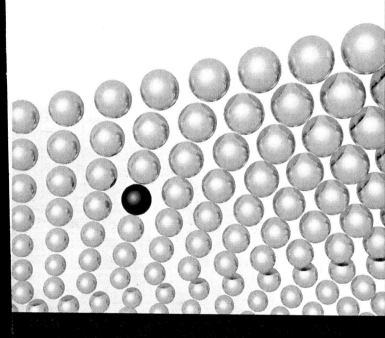

(r)evolution heirs
work peacefully together
with love and art hands

candle light in eyes
reflects histories enriched
by our ancestors

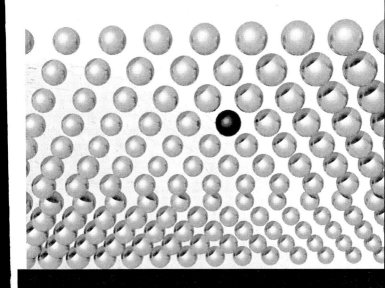

gentle strength begins
with a kiss in the morning
and a smile at night

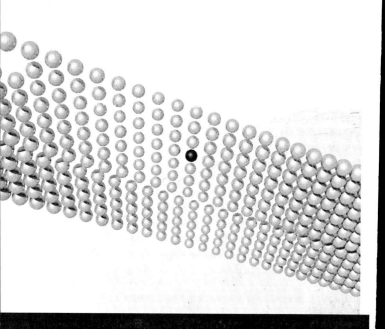

massaging your scalp
releases any harmful
stress throughout the day

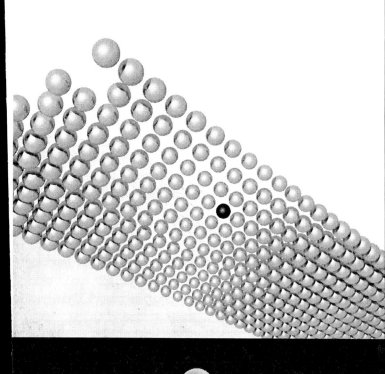

using video
between people and places
collapses distance

knowledge lands lightly
on a page without a doubt
of its potential

ghetto threads pierce lives
leaving superficial wounds
without moving [hearts]*
* parts

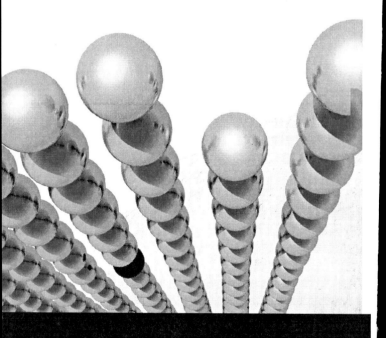

key tapping and beeps
sound for minutes but the wind's
play persists for hours

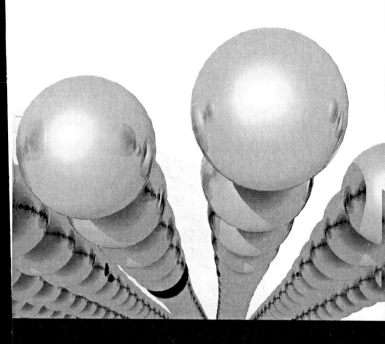

fingers on the floor
contemplate urban living
post supremacy

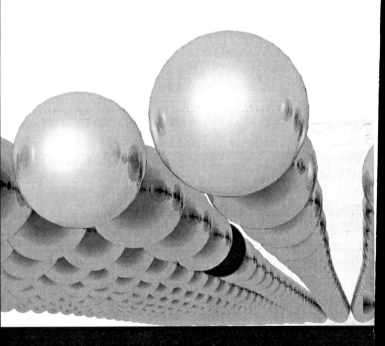

moving targets join
forces around three tables
pushing boundaries

eleven hours pass
around a cage without me
approaching its door

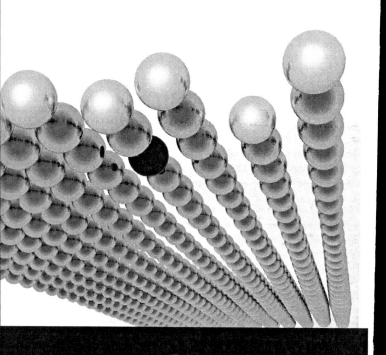

televised fury
slips in an exhale from lips
that have lost a stitch

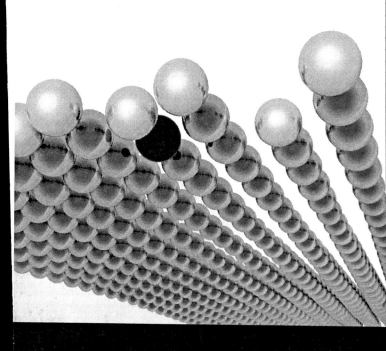

honesty rising
from self-adornment transcends
money and earns trust

hegemony twists
tid bits of self along streets
needing to be swept

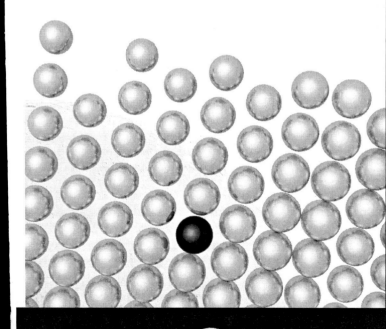

cycles continue
before the moon as witness
until voice moves hands

visual fissures
join supernumerary
desires mooning sand

resolved inflictions
self-direct new reception
without a worry

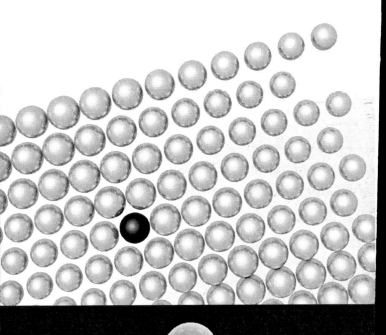

intuition serves
a new public laughter for
preparing actions

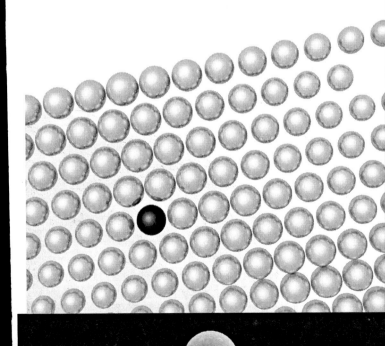

content sadness drives
commercial madness world wide
powering business

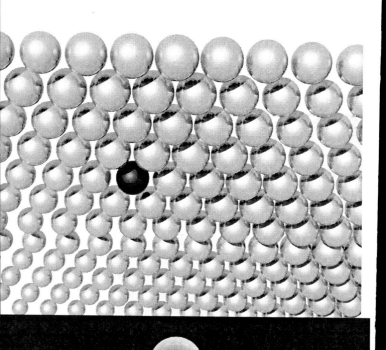

displaced families
challenge my complicity
releasing their pain

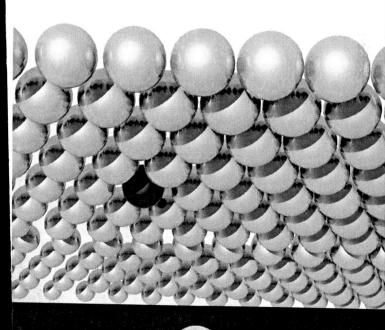

abundant options
arise from community
strategizing teams

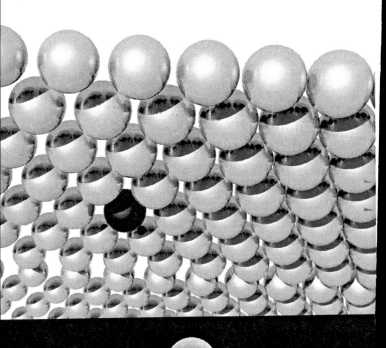

velocity solves
trickle down social justice
in broadcast networks

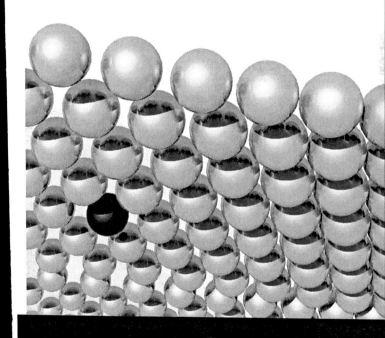

livin' and lovin'
self-identified power
is a silent space

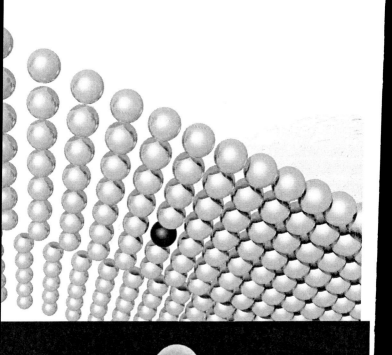

silent protests stream
tears ignored by smiling "cocks"
needing transition

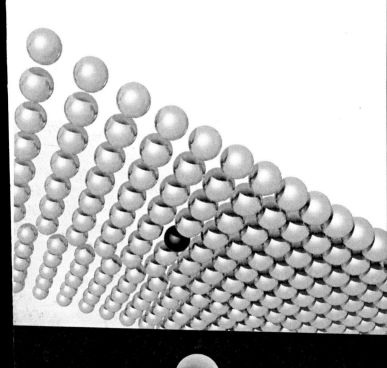

severe homeboys meet
on scattered intersections
throughout the city

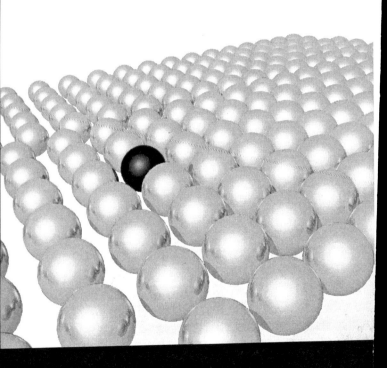

sleep deprivation
confuses priorities
preparing for work

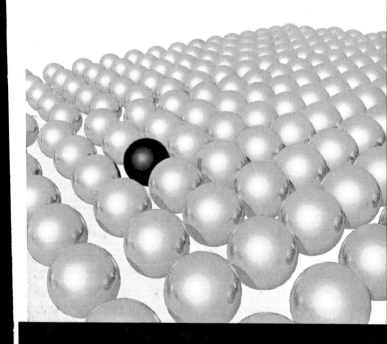

by hook or by crook
we gather to share in each
other's brave success

evolution thrives
in our flesh and memory
presently at peace

tribal gatherings
transgress physical limits
imposed by bodies

poleward pandemic
pansexualities peace
people playfully

mestiza artists
organize exhibition
challenging viewers

haunted pale figures
long to be free of the past
yet persist killing

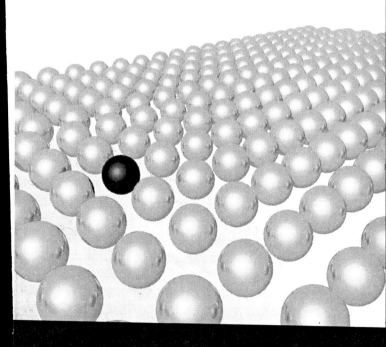

grassroot strategists
convene with all networks crossed
ready for big change

galleries promote
"art" reflecting wealthy lives
during recessions

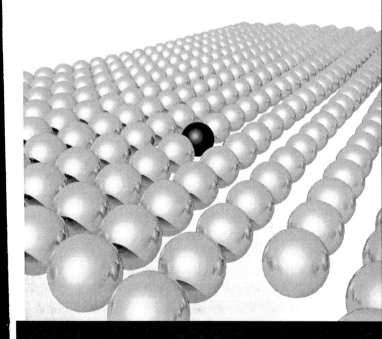

family and friends
continue to inspire love
without exception

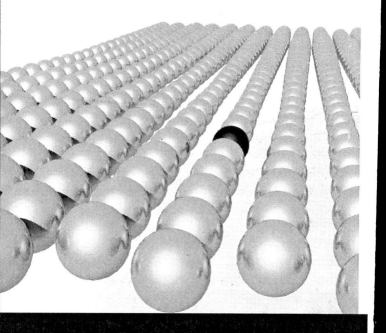

young urban queer whore
walks all night to pay the rent
and buy some water

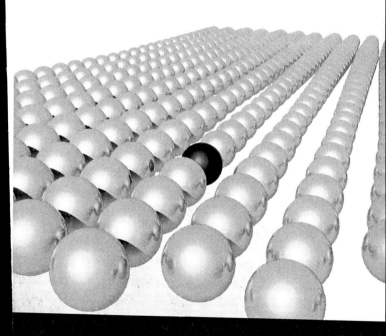

cactus transport fuels
nationalist holiday
travel secretly

mourning lost dollars
fails an honest working class
in education

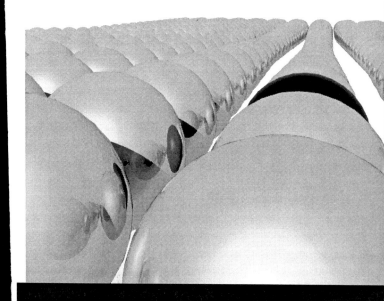

five colored boys play
rituals of love making
with q-poc* support
* queer people of color

sensitivities
gather from around the world
sharing words for love

an empty dwelling
retains displaced affections
needing attention

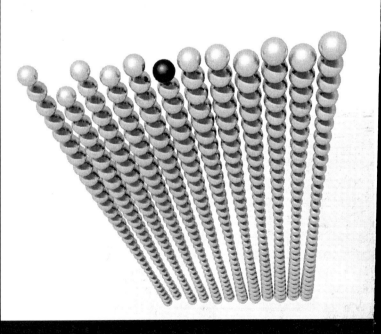

drunken lapse ceases
in shower recognizing
opportunities

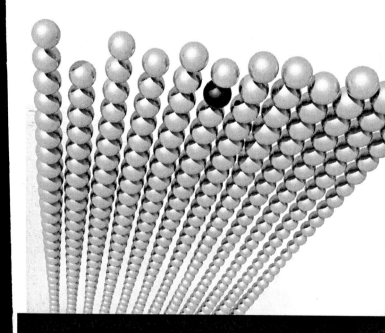

housing projects shift
location within meaning
from past to present

pleasant surprises
renew commitments to friends
and loving gestures

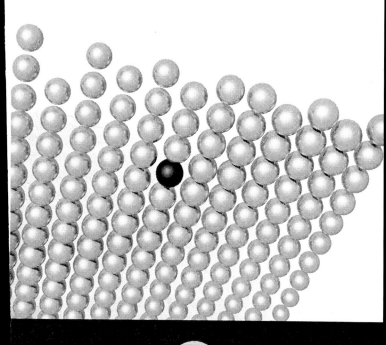

recognition streams
unfold painful decisions
postponing the truth

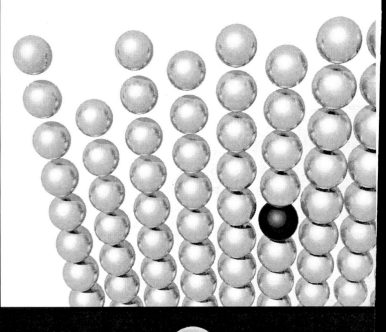

numbness fades quickly
mientras haciendo caras
within my aztlan

commercial madness
pounds relentlessly on lives
(tw)itching to break free

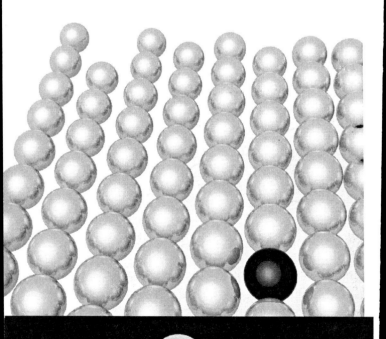

a third kind kiss calms
emotional turbulence
inspired by tension

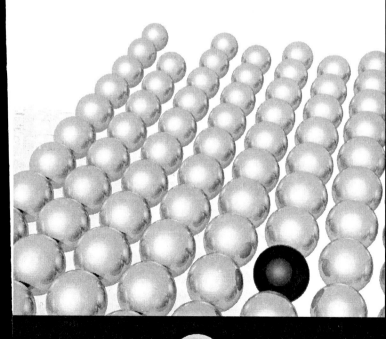

fruitful loved ones bring
innovative strategies
together at once

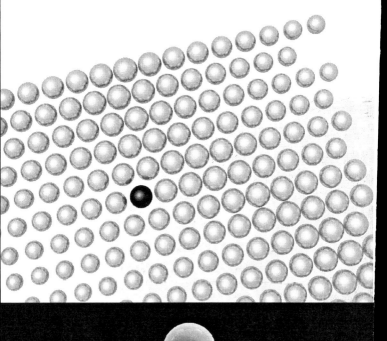

unpopular deeds
only remain so until
they're popularized

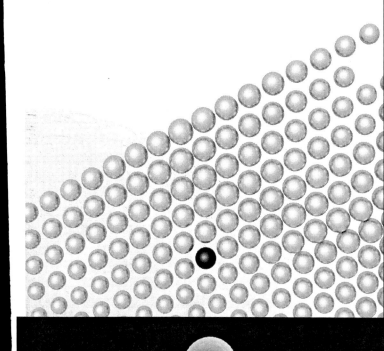

transparent values
provide greater incentive
to decolonize

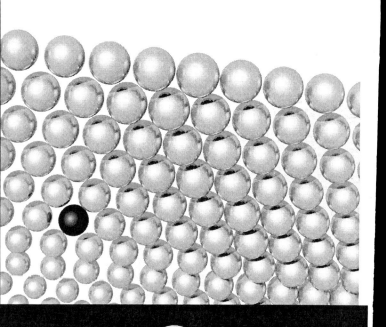

natural rhythms
traverse cultural structures
destined to crumble

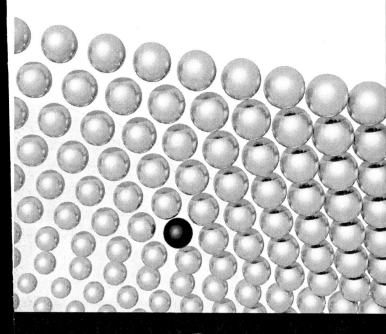

listening to friends
silently on peaceful walks
sharing food lessons

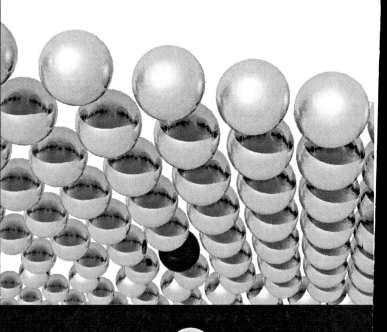

forgotten words play
mental images gathered
weaving throughout town

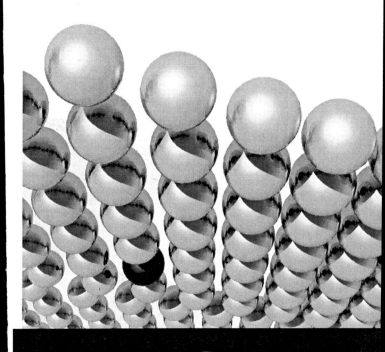

poisonous seeds hold
karma's secret from my neck
released in kindness

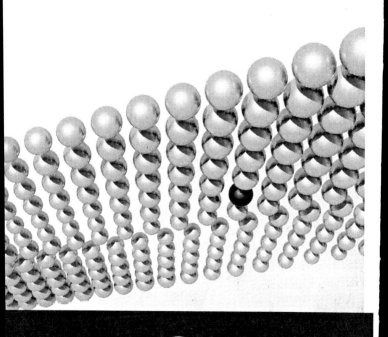

atypical moves
allow moods to settle down
while in loud settings

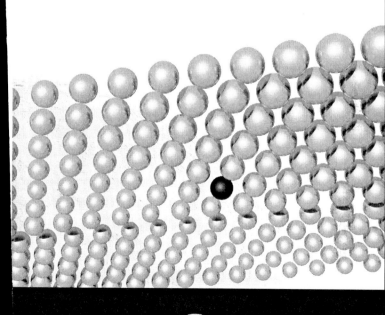

lives in transition
confront centuries of words
constructed for slaves

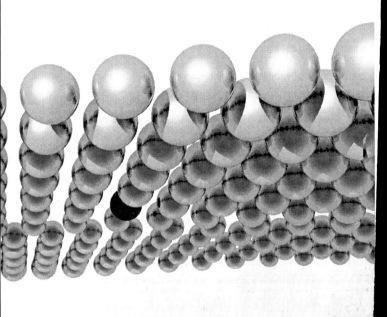

a bundle of sticks
stamped 'past due' sits quietly
amidst night movements

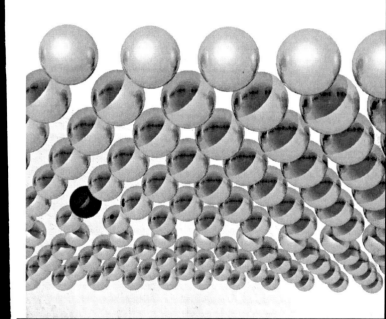

post party decor
frames queeruptive exchanges
intending to grow

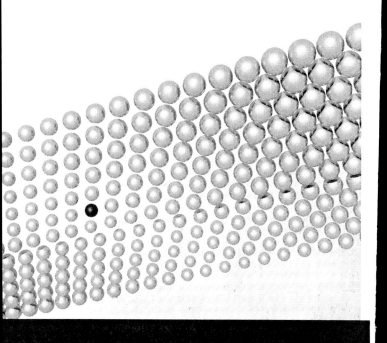

organic food high
invites images of depth
near windows and doors

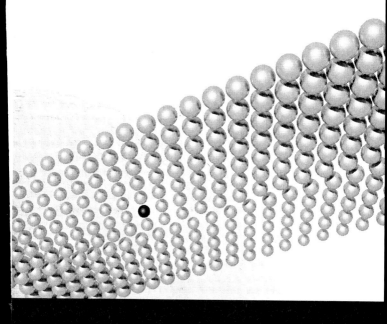

private bus ride slides
humiliation in red
down blonde public stairs

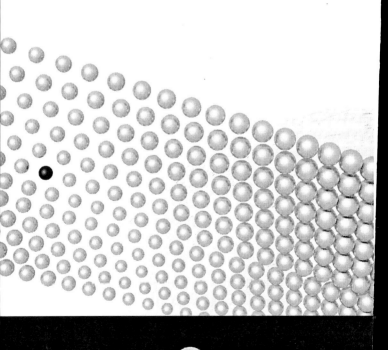

eyelids wet by lips
honor summer solstice beats
breaking vicious ruts

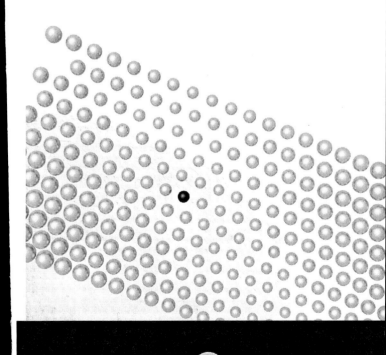

sister love beauty
be first to yourself and heal
all the pain he's caused

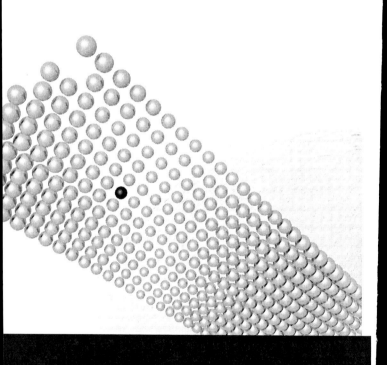

queer pride slogan links
menacingly corporate
goals with our pockets

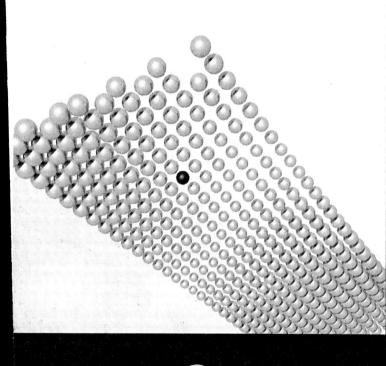

though asked not to cry,
tears stream releasing hinged dreams
otherwise ignored

gentle bells sound work
break for one while others start
their shift on the streets

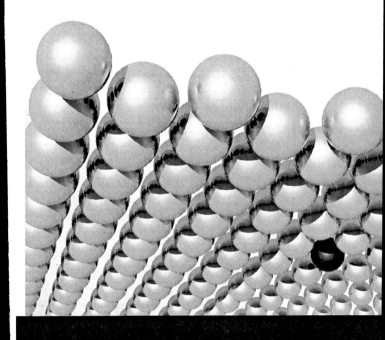

quality time sparks
laughter in letting narrow
people go their way

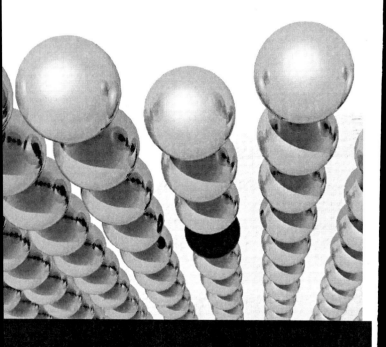

dumpster crossings fill
visual plane with warm hearts
carrying large smiles

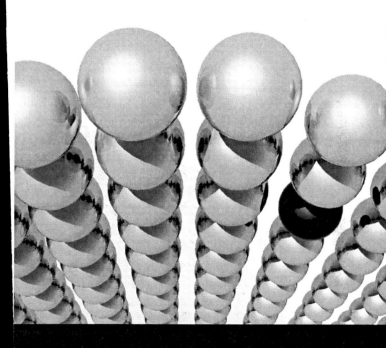

history conflates
"let them eat you take the cake"
super sonic mass

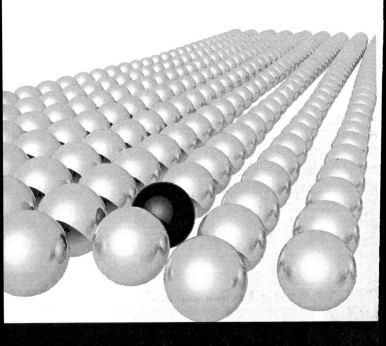

release of signals
calms mindful expectations
while eyes rest their lids

tender transitions
relinquish rigid remains
sparing self-abuse

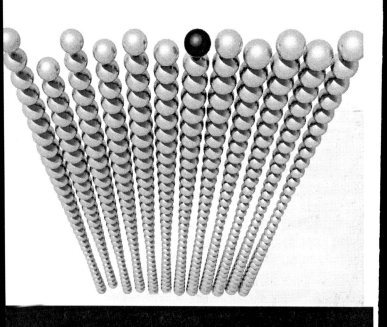

quarter thrill seekers
loop feverishly about
knots coming undone

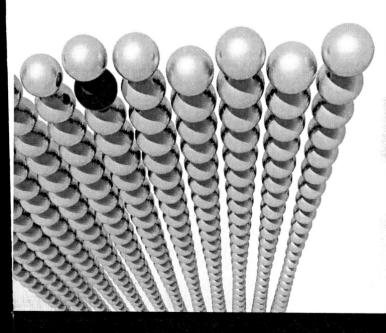

cultural traumas
subside upon deciding
the war is over

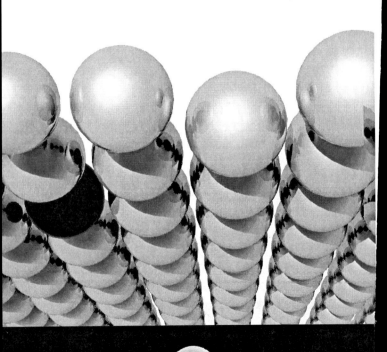

infused tenderness
halts careless mind rotations
despite gravity

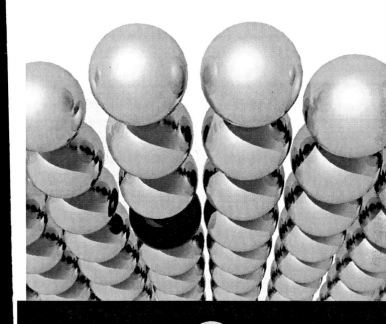

lunar perfect waves
reduce urgers to small spots
ready for cleaning

trusting young children
seek affection from adults
watching videos

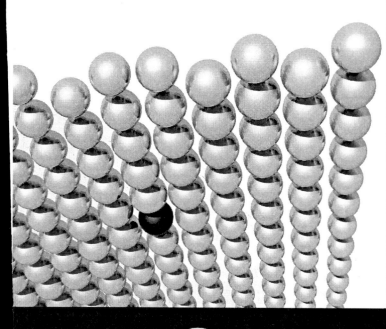

shipyard antics merge
friendships with the fast lane coach
on car rides through town

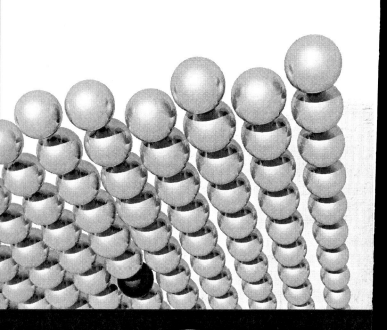

gentle words of love
exchanged right before slumber
awaken the mind

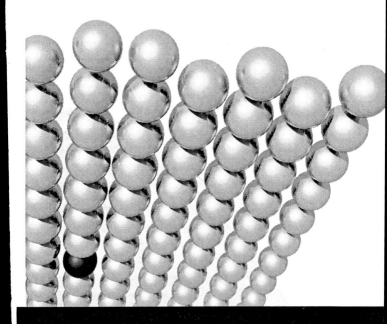

undoing trauma
over long conversations
questions intentions

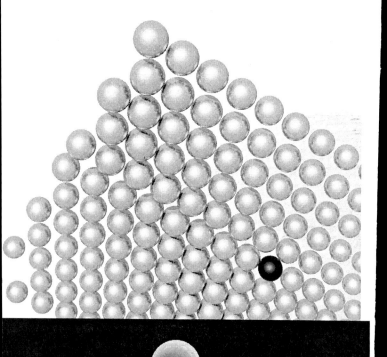

feathers speak for hours
harmonizing subtle shifts
required of mountains

three choices stir fire
longing to write blinking thoughts
while lifting glasses

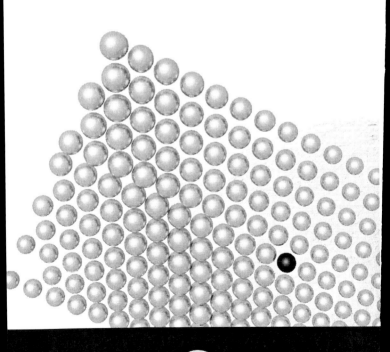

framed conversations
melt family barriers
imposed by conquest

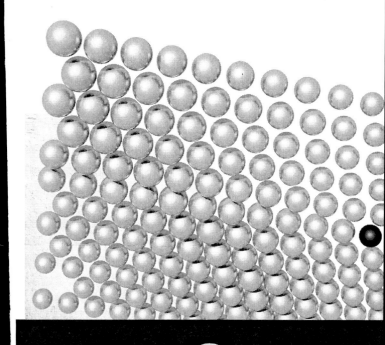

flickering candles
heighten strong pouncing shadows
against moving lips

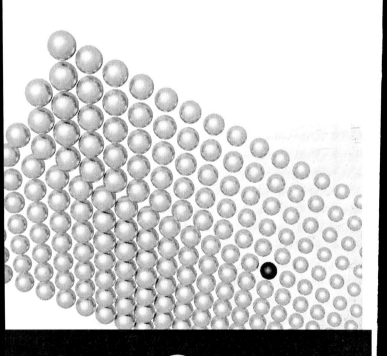

post-stagnation flight
frightens tired protectionists
freeing new signals

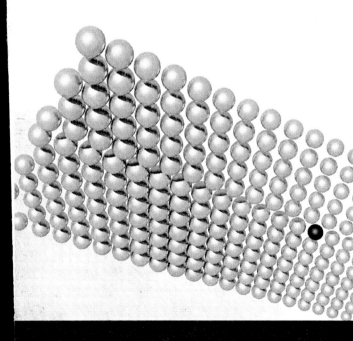

morning walls reflect
thoughts collected playfully
upon departure

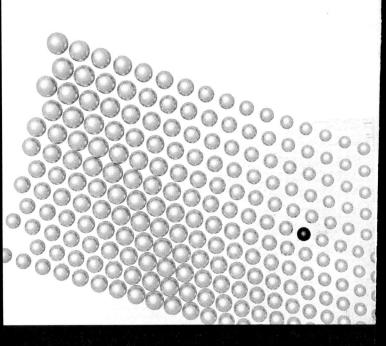

-one minutes
nout writing a word
id i get anxious

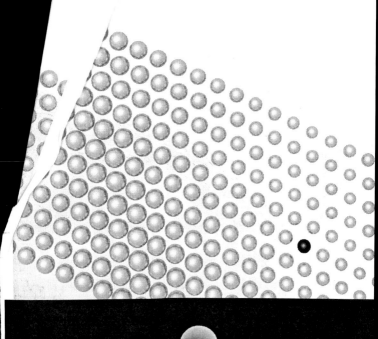

hard boy glances scare
those in the mirror at home
practicing alone

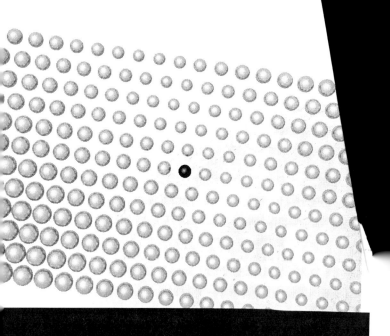

rationalized acts
cease being so rational
when people suffer

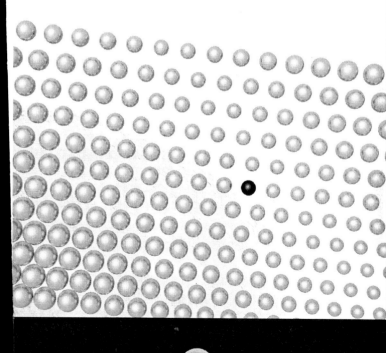

gentle brush strokes fade
swiftly weaving memories
over hardwood floors

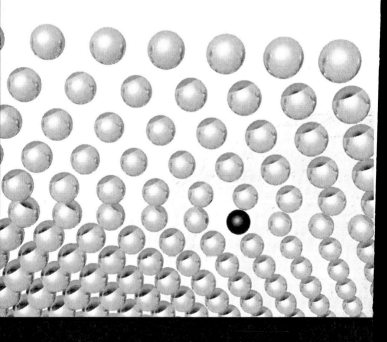

space entertains thoughts
shelved on supermarket aisles
awaiting purchase

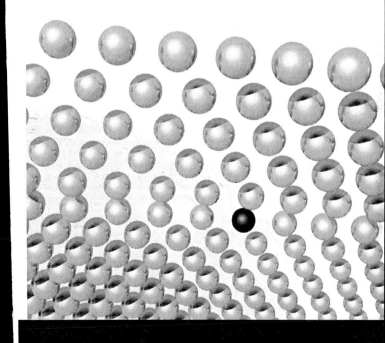

minor adjustments
release temporal bubbles
ready-made to burst

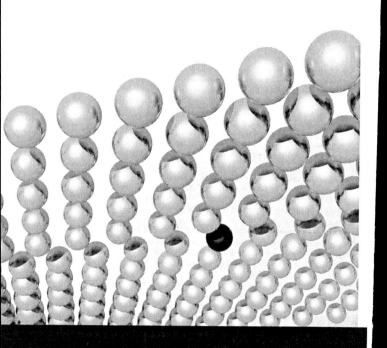

abrupt departures
endure desire's paved distance
beyond poverty

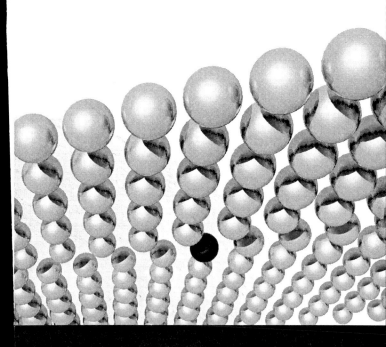

white drug dealers crowd
entrance to popular bar
pushing narcotics

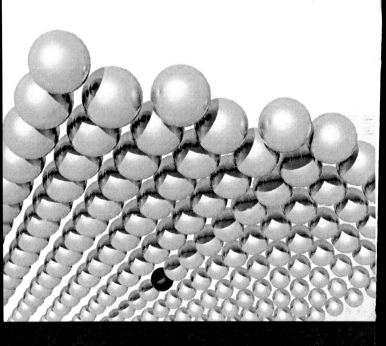

wind swept tunnel trips
replay invites to expand
beyond mass cult sites

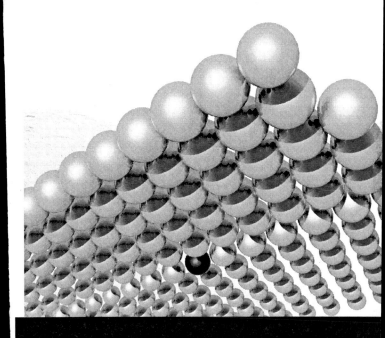

disconnected souls
feed on empty promises
lit by flashing bulbs

soft breadths imagine
lifestyle changes remaining
extra-sensory

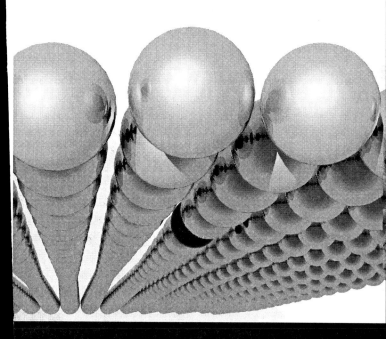

friendship offerings
light altars with warm gestures
sparked by love and art

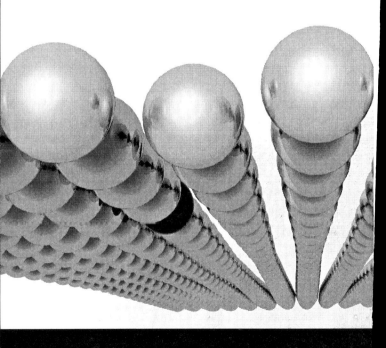

rythmik sounds echo
warm smiles in conversation
understanding needs

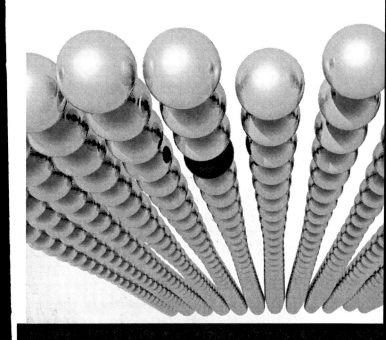

fragile voices span
a hillside's laconic stretch
searching for a place

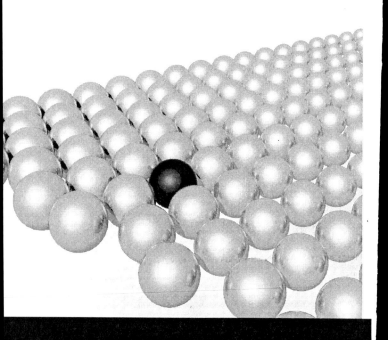

reflection amounts
contradictions voiced clearly
among radicals

art eco-systems
relate community needs
in various forms

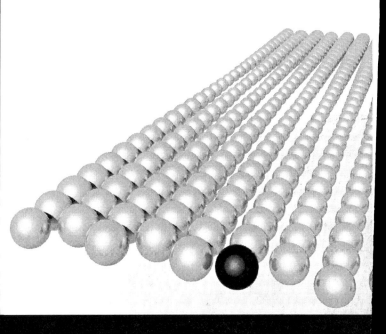

synthesized thoughts stream
history's cadent influx
while clearing out home

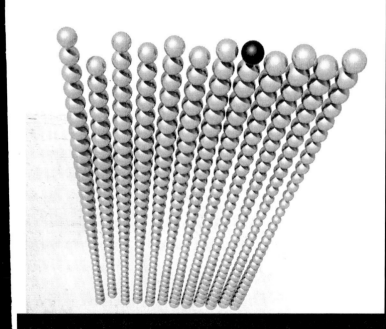

centered axis spins
memories kindly gathered
awaiting answers

exploitative ways
surface between sips of wine
passing lips of men

deafening constructs
cease all articulation
with pen on paper

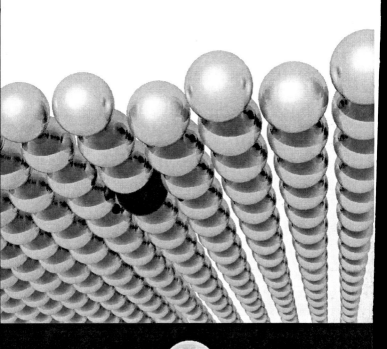

sexual questions
fluster a carload of men
braving a new world

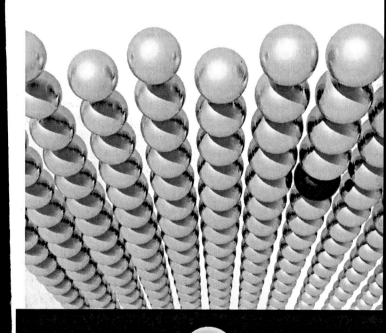

regional growth lifts
spirits speaking of travel
found in minds and hearts

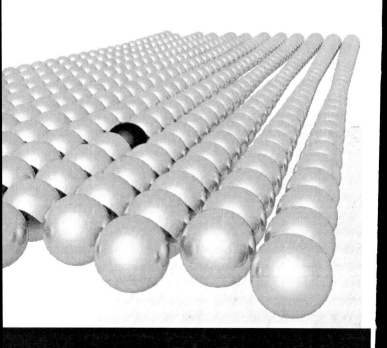

placement rituals
besiege all comprehension
despite location

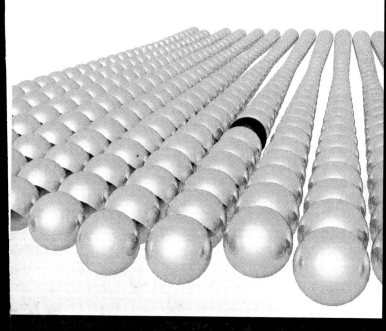

mental sifting shakes
rigid thoughts to the surface
ready for kindness

scattered images
recombine on street corners
creating new life

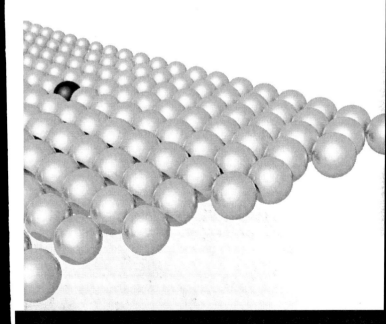

patiently sitting
the sun sets crowns for flying
outside my window

living galaxies
convene bodies graciously
sharing high love tones

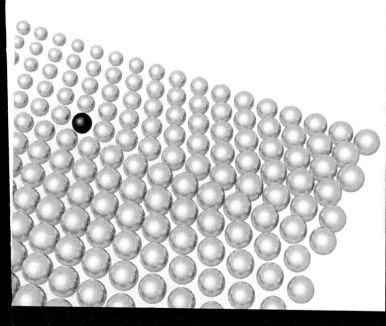

flickering red walls
illuminate street corners
chosen by sirens

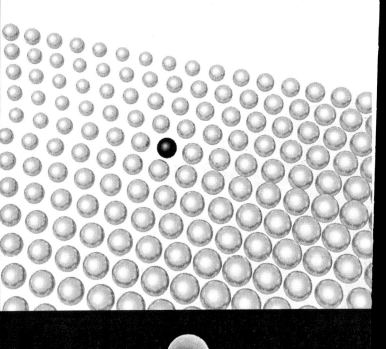

plastic bag remnants
occupy needle and thread
ready for transit

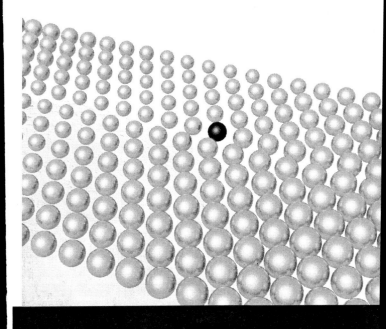

electric city
hookers walk the misty streets
paved with wild magic

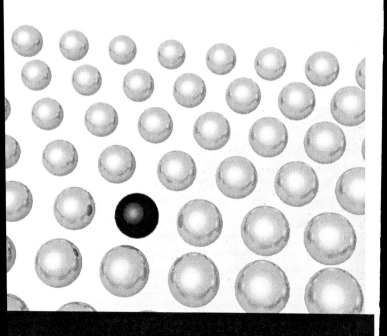

break through vibrations
assemble complete beings
seeking nourishment

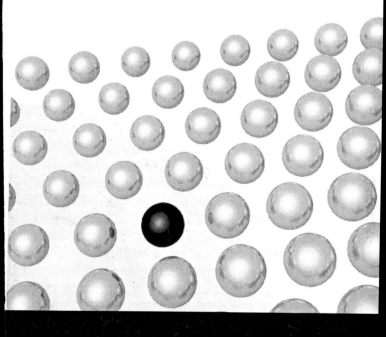

soulful connections
extend beats over meaning
intimating space

shooting star gazers
streetwalk with interlocked arms
running from shadows

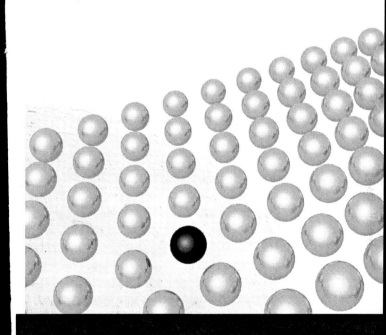

mi-wuk ancestors
offer guidance through gesture
attached to legends

revolution holds
bodies gently intertwined
in seeds at harvest

video shoes breathe
interconnectivity
striking consciousness

surprise encounters
disintegrate high culture
as time circulates

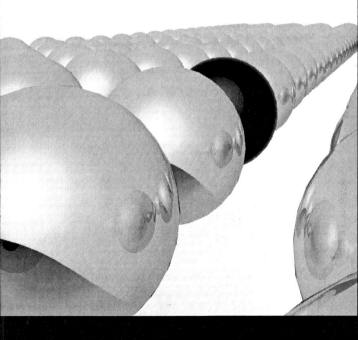

sabotage quintet
disbands upon changing tune
through glitter sequence

shared intuition
ceases perfection debates
imposed by light skin

american piles
unfold cyclical sirens
collapsing time/space

da da da da da
da da da da da da da
da da da supremes

post-traumatic stress
re-televises itself
while the screen is on

feather love turns thoughts
combining multiple planes
raising our voices

salty kombu bath
dissolves isolation scripts
threatening system

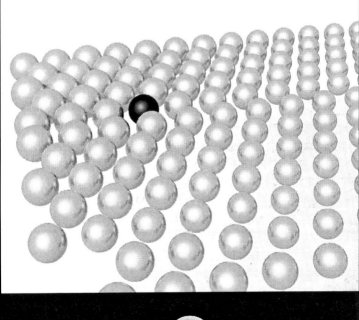

charged sounds carry heads
oscillating bound bodies
found in light tracings

faculties center
extra ordinary spin
cycle cleansing cells

byproduct babies
orbit pink conversations
devoid of feeling

final episodes
counter established regimes
in dis-placing fear

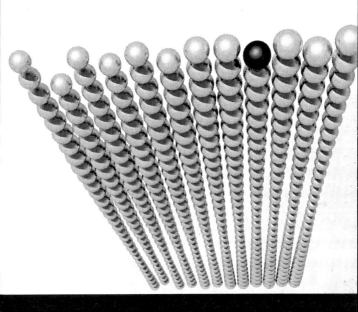

moments of silence
bolster the courage to hear
gentle vibrations

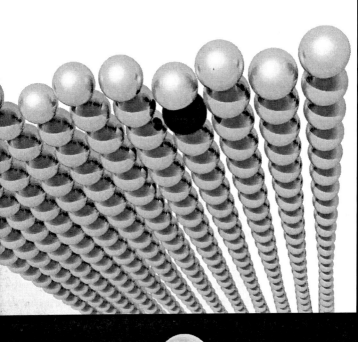

outdated models
question lost accuracies
informing current

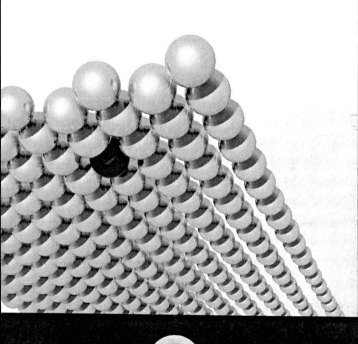

bodies in waiting
socialize accordingly
until a break down

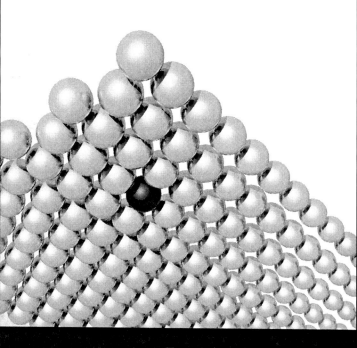

green stitching circles
slide dreaming cow reminders
under metal bars

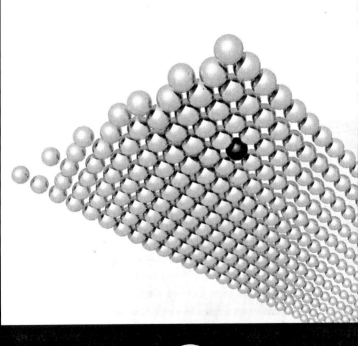

finger swept karma
springs seeds with lips and warm hands
speaking of loved ones

living stains whisper
history's uncertain facts
written between lines

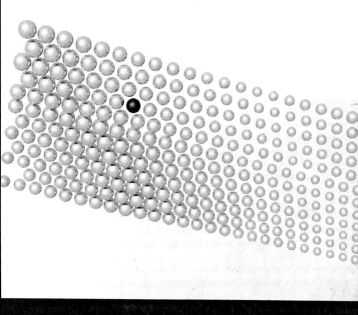

reflection rattles
window thinking about friend
attempting her death

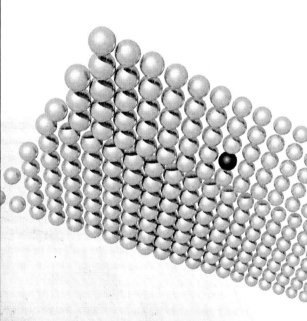

spaces between clouds
still empty thoughts behind doors
remaining open

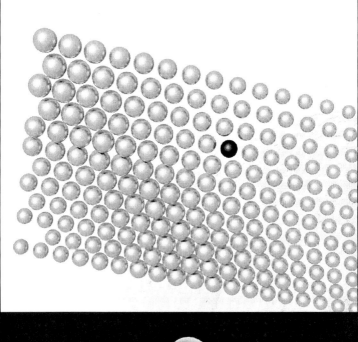

phone conversations
expound thematics of love
in battle for peace

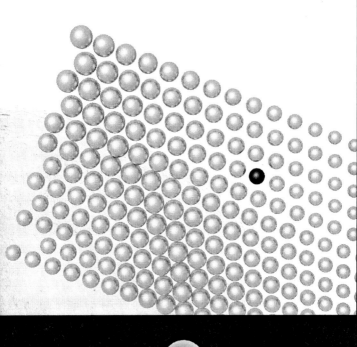

human struggles raise
white national legacies
up for scrutiny

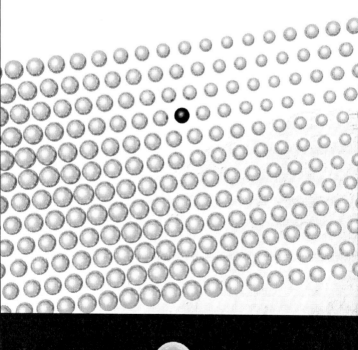

sun reminder halts
colonialist abuses
directed at self

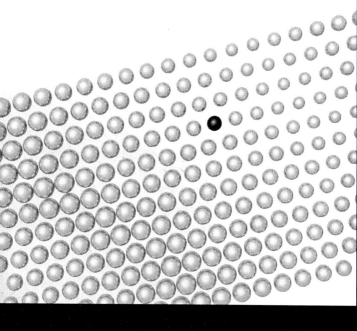

sounds of sleep carry
soul thoughts of ending racism
into this moment

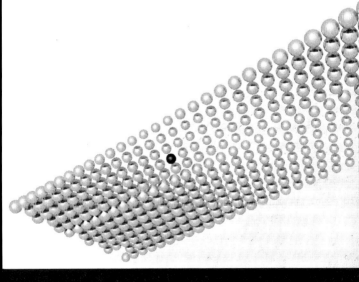

present hands the past
promises of reflection
ready for action

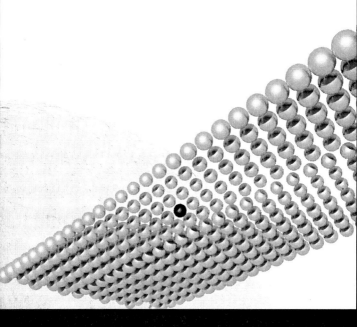

cards of intention
integrate releasing depths
yet completely seen

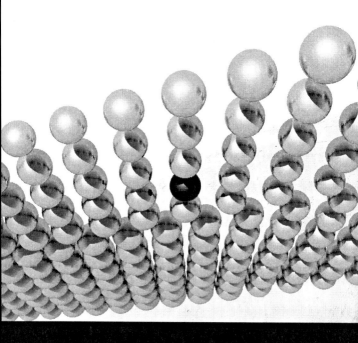

amber waves of fame
nurture momentous amor
equally throughout

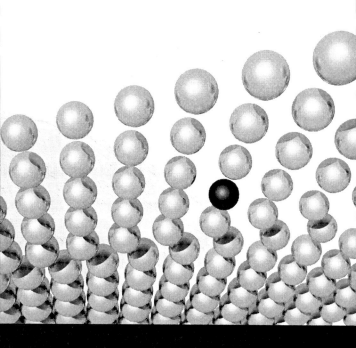

limitations sway
riding buses across town
in search of agent

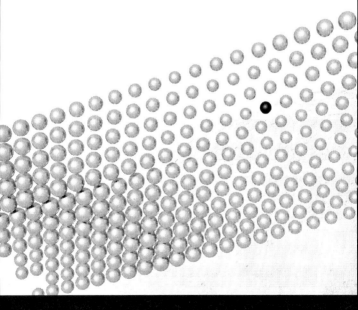

raised heads locate hearts
full of like desire and schemes
flowing rhythmic vibes

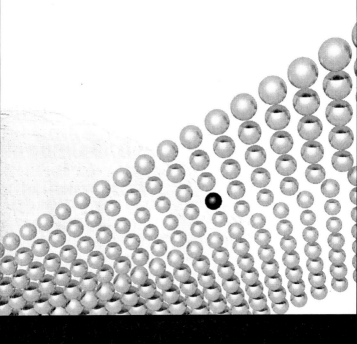

kind invitations
establish work connections
in the universe

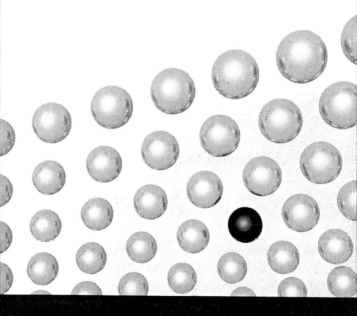

zodiac thrillers
deconstruct violent strides
before the last trains

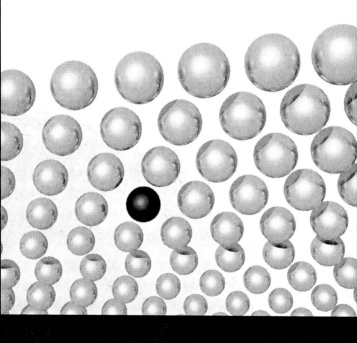

three monitors raise
community health concerns
central to day's work

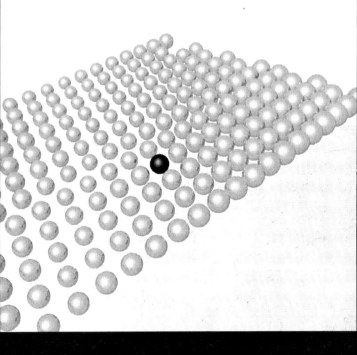

star quality knows
media punishment serves
capital culture

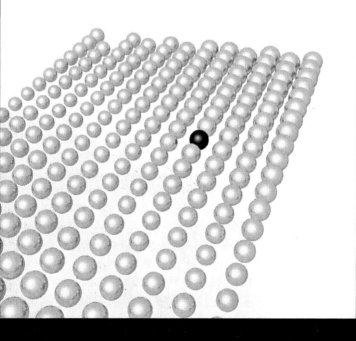

fevered conflation
thrusts living manifesto
towards total s[p]a[c]e

in hour reflection
specificity falters
while wetting large trees

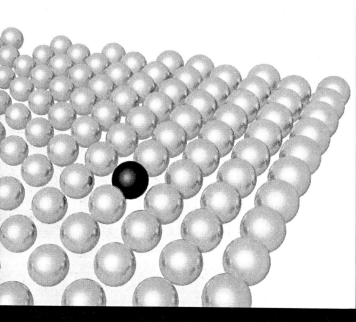

flutter formations
followed for fascination
free philosophies

young american
clichés deteriorate
cross culturally

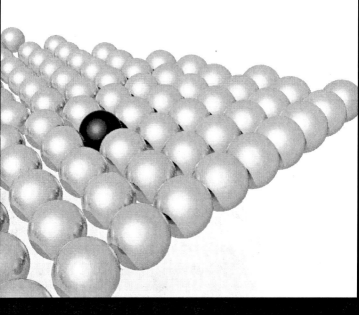

swept napkins circle
before another attack
transforms my silence

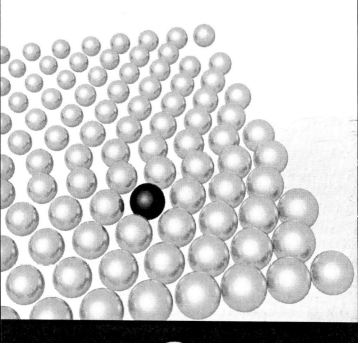

muffled bruises throb
yet beauty insists on love
in every moment

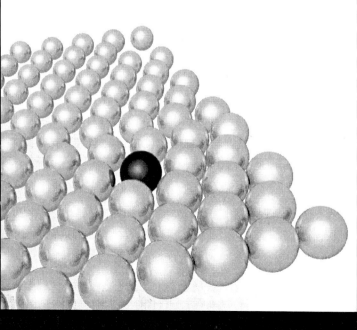

village centered talk
extends family circles
without delusions

relentless living
beguiles insightful breathing
before remembrance

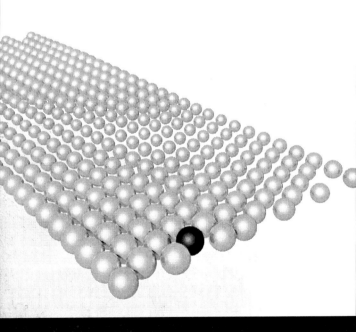

underground movements
surface past and future friends
warding off evil

attentive minds hand
tele-gram-type reminders
licking juicy lips

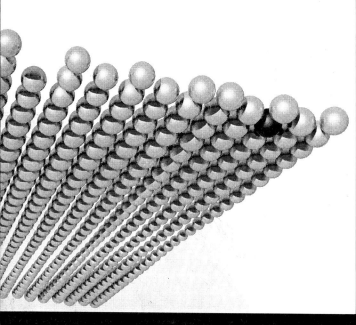

walk on the wild side
gathers moments across time
linked to performance

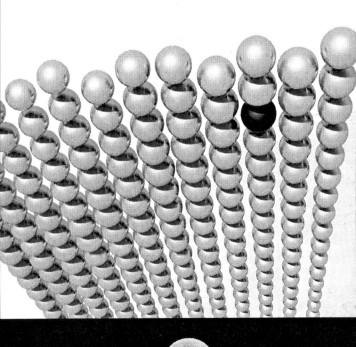

music strings flashback
pre-recorded traumata
post."white dick" bus ride

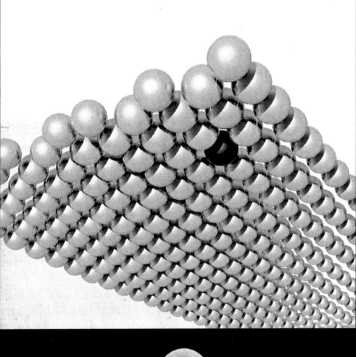

key pad fingers probe
questions of functionalism
short of a mir'cle

change scraped destiny
awakens multi-use vibes
defying diction

friends in orange melt
slide along hand held plastic
dropping aural forms

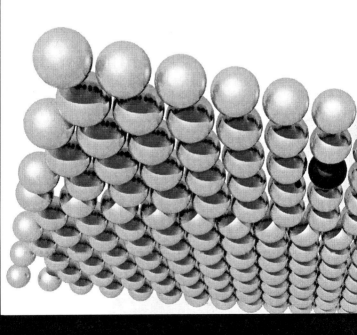

industrial waste
sweetens blue cellophane bait
cast over concrete

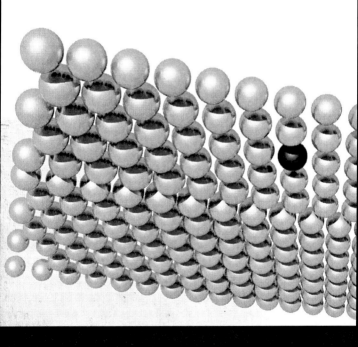

overt narrative
tendencies crumble slowly
clinging to power

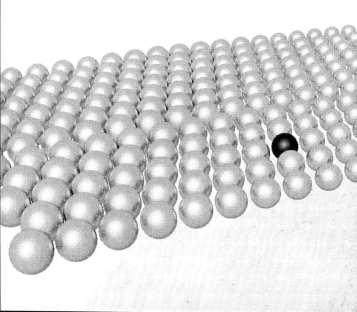

testimonies cure
isolationist dogmas
saturating thought

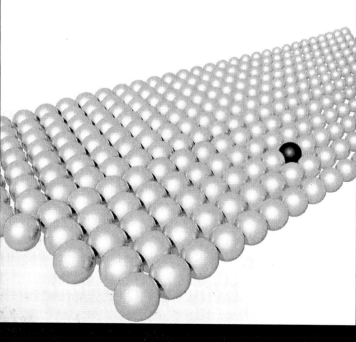

fragrant beginnings
coalesce before dogged flames
calling upon dawn

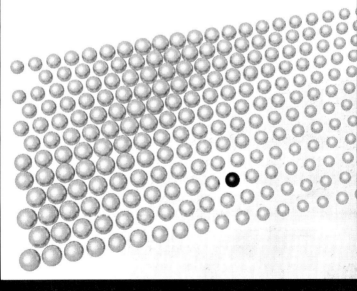

gentle hand on thigh
brings a tender smile to eyes
longing to touch back

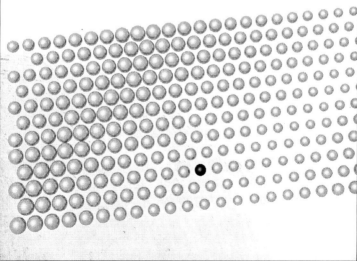

vanishing chair stirs
advice against becoming
what is criticized

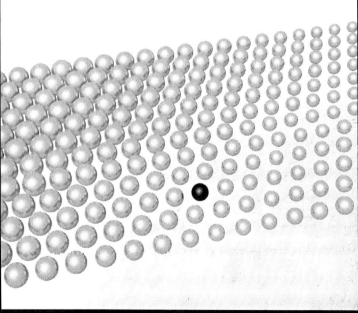

ultra baroque lives
suddenly within high walls
beaming projections

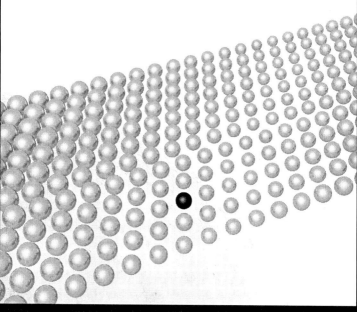

gentle exchanges
amidst turbulent designs
eases suffering

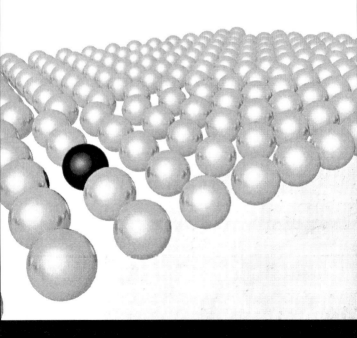

stomach water splash
relieves all anxiety
when not expected

exposed pink circles
tickle smiles leaping from air
repeating lyrics

lost and found public
displays reformulations
bound in tradition

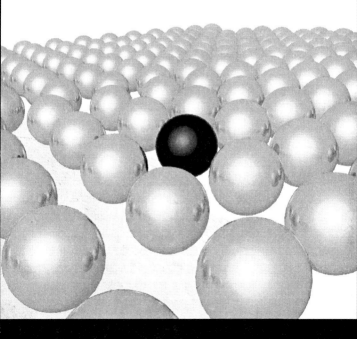

chronic instance drops
hold of cultural demands
transgressing moon dance

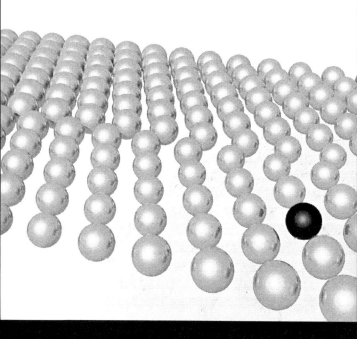

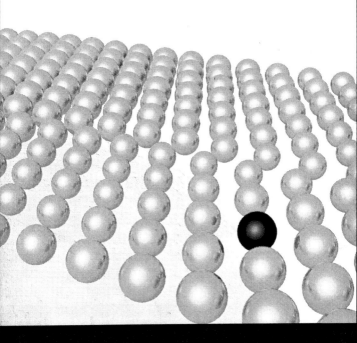

displaced objectives
collect the scent of onion
re-inscribing home

apparent corners
release stones from common tasks
merging mirror drives

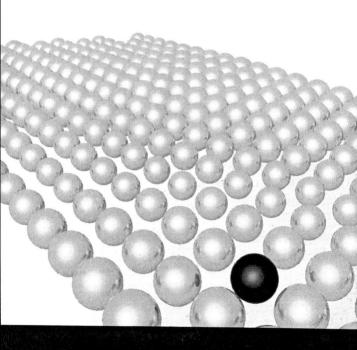

overlaps nourish
relationships filtering
afflictive static

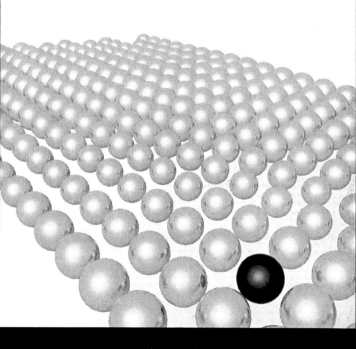

improvised risk shifts
technocratic gaze bravely
committed to love

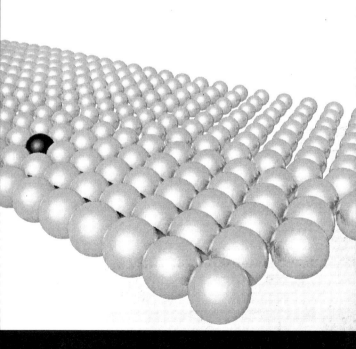

waves radio fresh
queer ghetto urbanity
moving bound headphones

double take day joins
rhythmik flow of karmic sounds
speaking to spirits

friendships conquer jails
built to contain our people
after all these years

circle sorts paper
painstakingly shedding hate
re-reading love notes

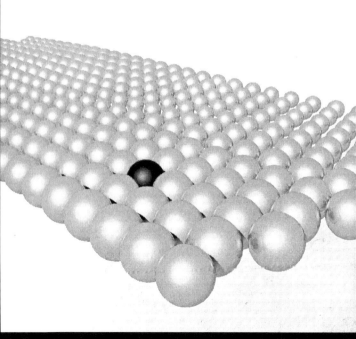

from high to super
performance signs realize
romance department

exhaustion trinkets
dissolve well in rain water
following a laugh

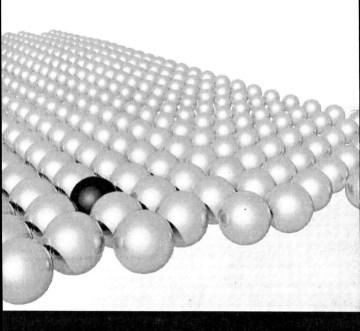

underground systems
surface pretty worldly men
playing with desire

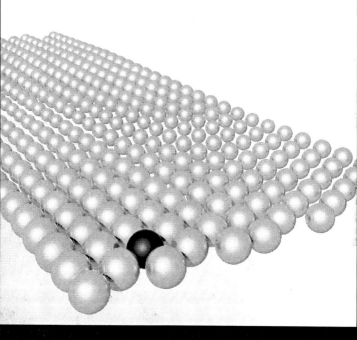

sunny companion
double plays a frame of night
moving in orbits

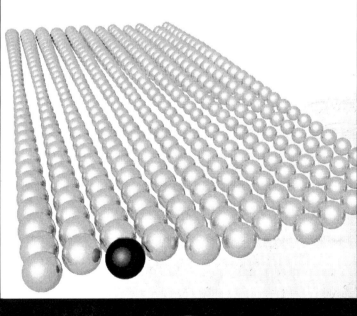

orange intentions
beat, breathe, walk and write life force
listening past sounds

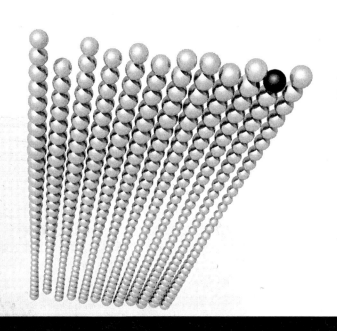

ancestor queer looks
compute political streams
splicing into dreams

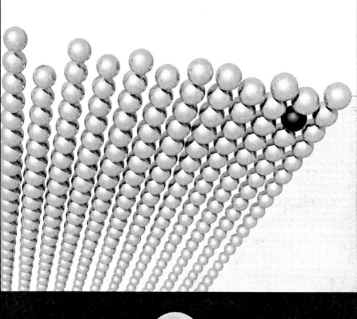

random acts of love
ease stress related tension
from head to shoulders

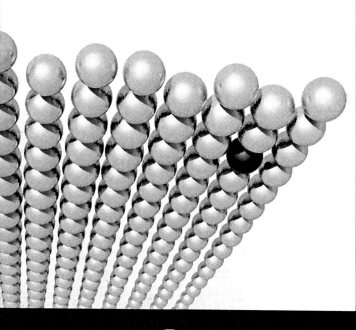

exposed light bulb thoughts
remove narrative's green web
short of energy

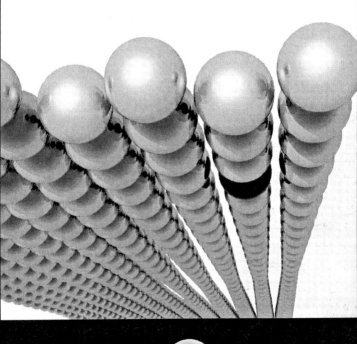

semi-quarter lapse
toe wiggler near white surface
lives internal drive

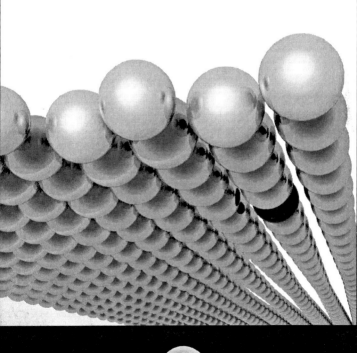

street corners perform
elements found underground
framed by queer reading

slip knots discount stores
coughing leaves along pavement
not forgetting words

mistaken order
out serves poor business practice
in former clubland

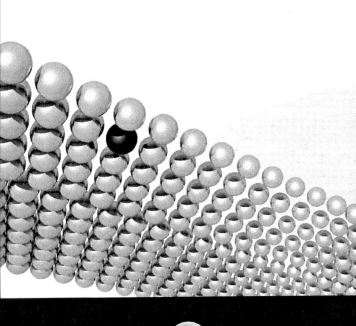

organic thoughts stream
blues connections to public
city art model

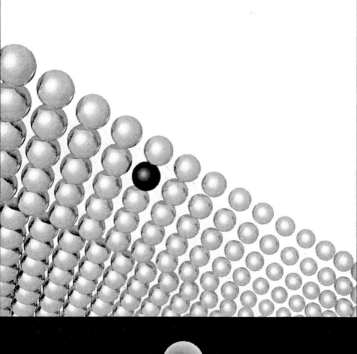

digi-slam display
impatiently half-waiting
along the curbside

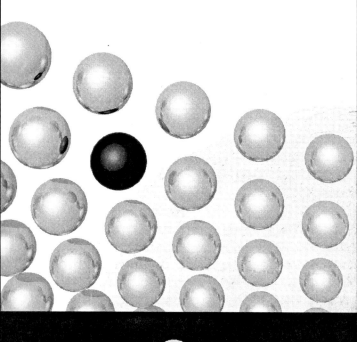

pocho talk times two
devoid of geography
connects sunday lips

emotional depths
(p)urge into the next era
exhibiting health

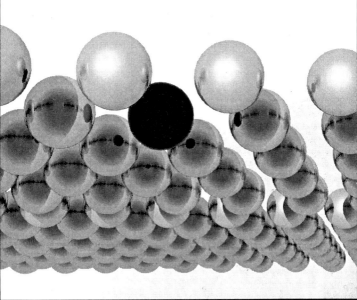

glowing currency
follows racist neighborhood
under discussion

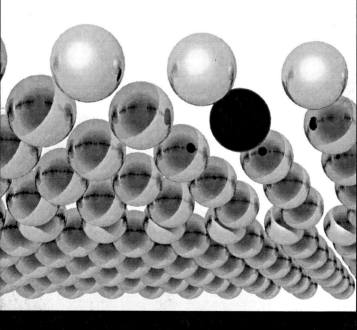

be-bop linguistics
fade semi-automatic
rotations on cue

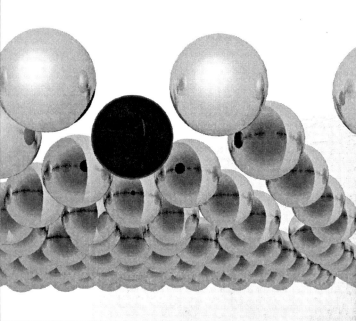

dot connections spray
shadows across new era
calling for big time

kwality timing
spins abstractions out of us
listening to noise

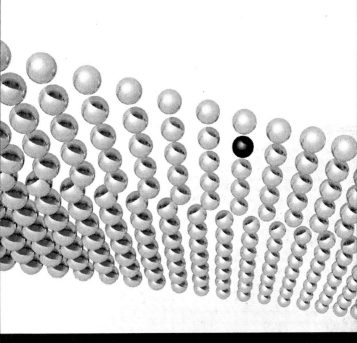

top heavy windows
find relief in agile hands
willing to take risks

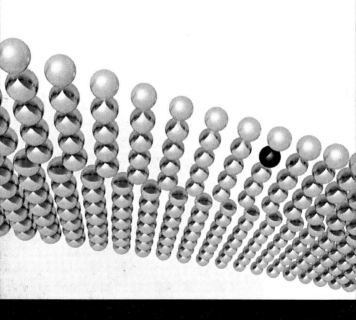

bus stop reflections
twist functional wave movements
bound to be released

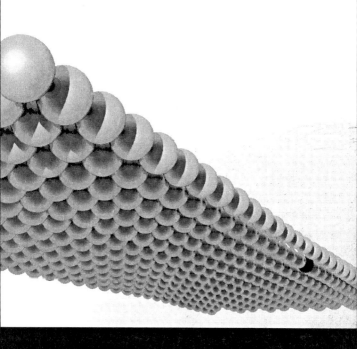

weather settles sense
closing eyelids to free art
without exception

distant voices bend
imaginary homelands
found by candlelight

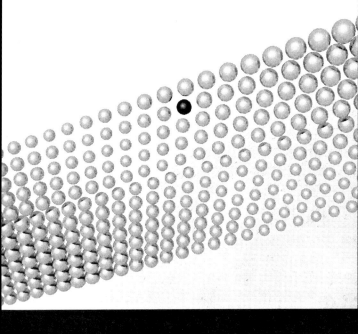

sublimated grief
speaks to wind through restless leaves
licking an artist

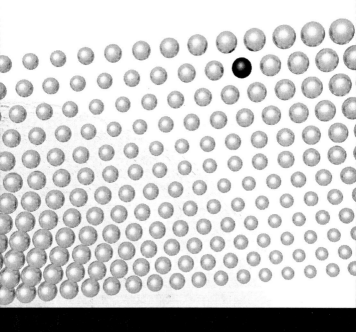

connections span home
invested in love shaping
thankfully grinning

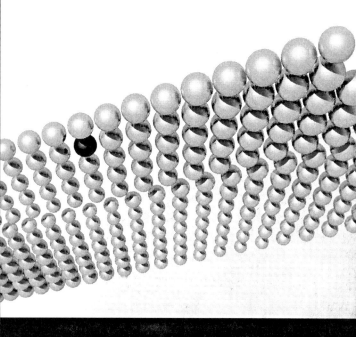

scenic darkness signs
brave transitory stillness
beating waves in time

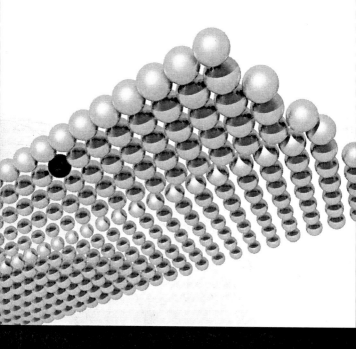

colonial sugar
sweetens bitterness grown on
other plantations

lingering pool prayer
eradicates short vision
brought on by conflict

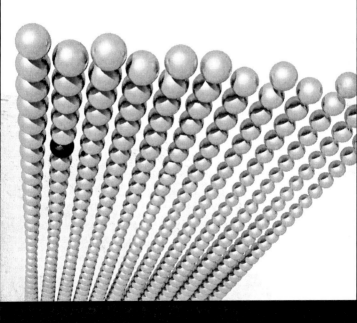

hungry crazy talk
prompts an examination
into everything

kiss to back of hand
lifts ink from a fertile (p)age
touching a warrior

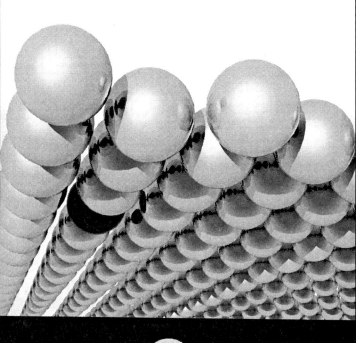

silent exchanges
follow intricate purpose
not easily seen

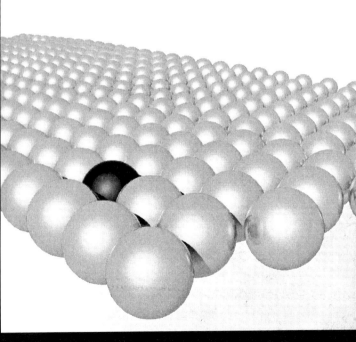

lunar reminders
speak from revolution's tongue
upon listening

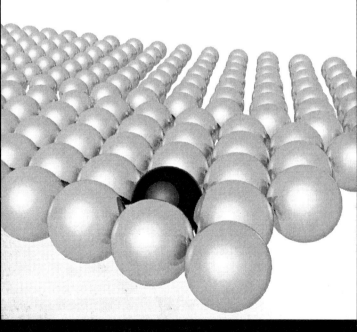

epoch industries
surround calls of love making
under rose petals

hooked up minds group lives
marking decade rotation
continued through sound

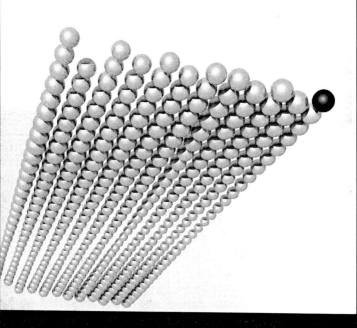

grateful hempsters spin
platform melodies in silk
weaving a tight knit

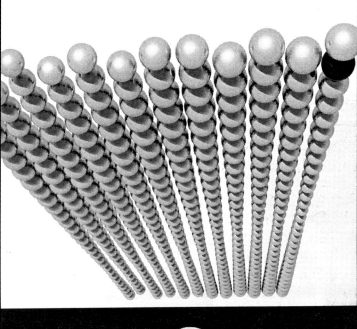

everyday lines spring
re-inventions in structure
flourishing real life

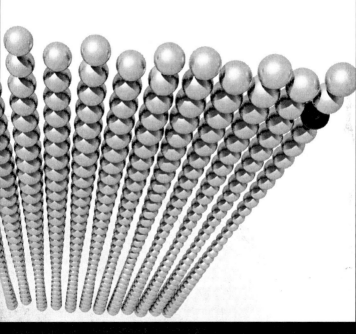

interculture straits
dissolve whiteness polemic
central to "science"

cathartic witness
deflects testimony's grain
timed uncertainly

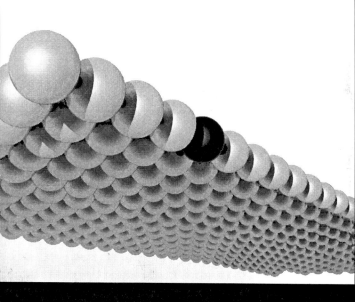

open city finds
public calling on clear screens
aimed toward all landmarks

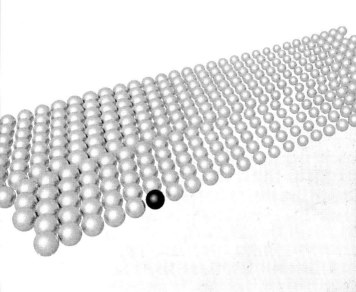

judgments listen in
while searching reminder blurs
distance artists fear

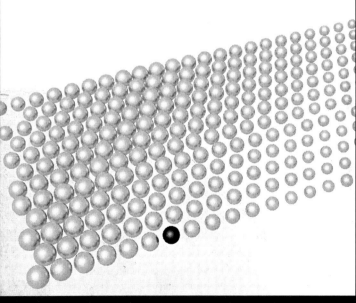

crescent in-dwellers
shape beauty in hostile times
tracing new visions

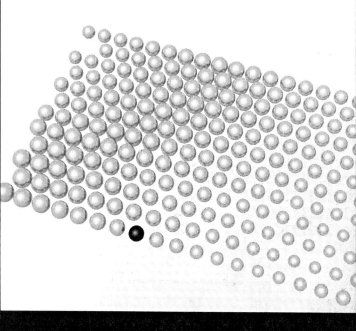

thermal influence
inspires tenderness in state
reducing all stress

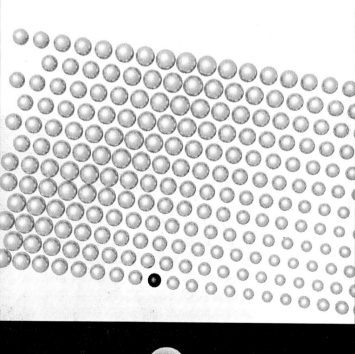

infinity floats
beyond town on giant plains
within plastic bags

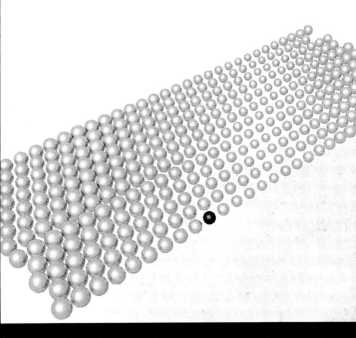

late night excursions
frame existential questions
surrounded by books

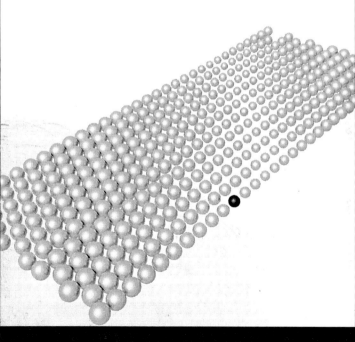

inter-power play
splits off in two directions
thumping civic beats

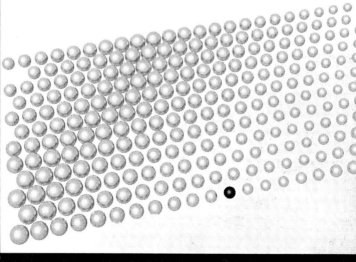

delinquent accounts
blank vital literacy
as nomenclature

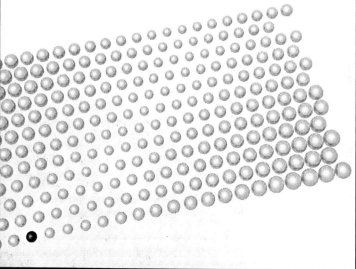

gangster interludes
interrupt complacent views
abandoning home

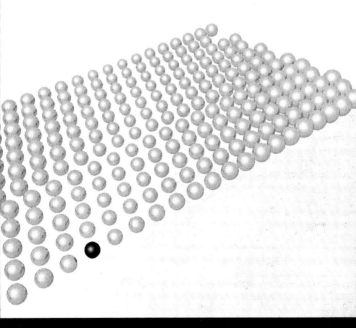

safety travels kill
art in retro-anti-work
fashion suspension

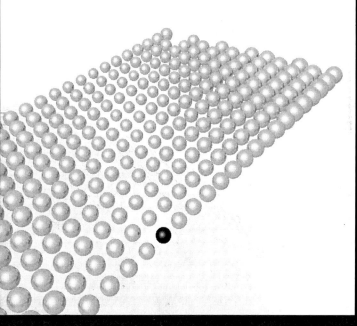

phonetic rain drops
wash away dire illusions
strewn from kitchen chairs

timid undertones
plague pale creative work funds
unable to serve

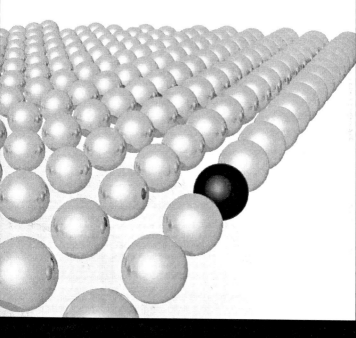

time watches drifters
unfolding profound landscapes
streaked with chemicals

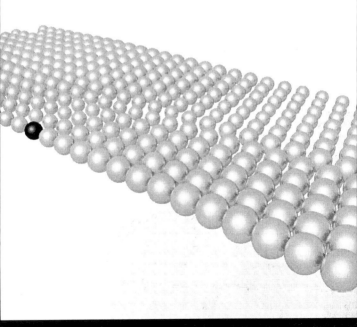

soft song trickles warmth
easing disparate visions
hidden behind grins

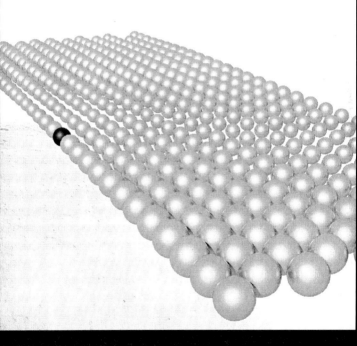

anticipation
postpones fulfillment in frames
without real meaning

displaced hands circle
wind patterns that rustle leaves
inviting rainfall

connecting smiles span
lifetimes found in books and bags
waiting for a shift

severe glass grinding
locates exit book-ended
with children of love

boundless tenderness
rocks bodies into morning
gaining perspective

partners improvise
ramble jumping to fun pads
in heightened dream state

layers fall from walls
preparing for family
gathering in art

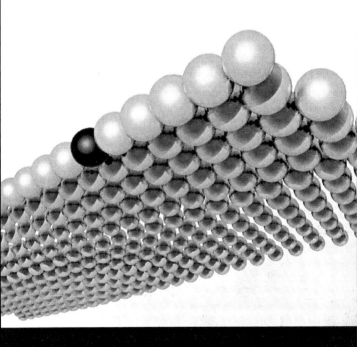

thankful moment drops
used bed to happy mountain
on post-memory

psychic healing thrives
within pumpkin kitchen talk
centered around play

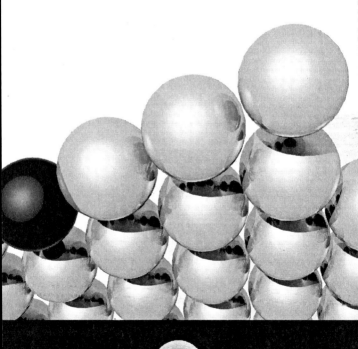

quilted words swing beats
in cards brought on by child songs
gone after sunset

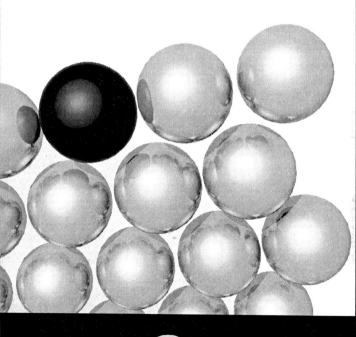

stubborn lines smile back
reflections of light in dreams
coiled ready to strike

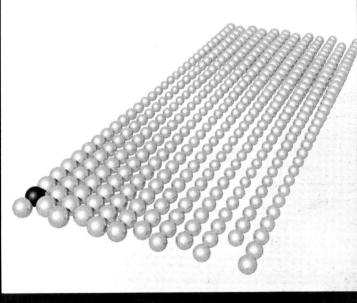

beauty unfolds self
walking peacefully along
admiring close friends

it's lunar...